THE
ASTROLOGY
DIARY
2026

ANA·LEO

THIS DIARY BELONGS TO

NAME
_____

DATE OF BIRTH _____ TIME _____

PLACE OF BIRTH _____ STATE _____

SOLAR SIGN _____ RISING SIGN _____

ADDRESS
_____

_____

CITY _____ STATE _____

COUNTRY
_____

PHONE _____ MOBILE _____

EMAIL
_____

WWW
_____

The Astrology Diary 2026

First published in the UK and USA
in 2025 by Watkins, an imprint of
Watkins Media Limited
Unit 11, Shepperton House,
89–93 Shepperton Road,
London N1 3DF

enquiries@watkinspublishing.co.uk

Commissioning Editor: Brittany Willis
Author: Ana Leo
Designers: Sarah O'Flaherty and
    Maria Clara Voegeli
Illustrations: Shutterstock

ISBN: 978-178678-962-4

Printed in China

Signs of the Zodiac:

♒	Aquarius	20 January–18 February
♓	Pisces	18 February–20 March
♈	Aries	20 March–20 April
♉	Taurus	20 April–21 May
♊	Gemini	21 May–21 June
♋	Cancer	21 June–22 July
♌	Leo	22 July–23 August
♍	Virgo	23 August–23 September
♎	Libra	23 September–23 October
♏	Scorpio	23 October–22 November
♐	Sagittarius	22 November–21 December
♑	Capricorn	21 December–20 January

Note: Zodiac signs change on the last
day shown for each sign. If you were
born on this day, refer to the Solar and
Lunar Calendar page for the exact time
of change.

www.watkinspublishing.com

The manufacturer's authorised
representative in the EU for product
safety is: eucomply OÜ - Pärnu
mnt 139b-14, 11317 Tallinn, Estonia,
hello@eucompliancepartner.com,
www.eucompliancepartner.com

Hello,

AND WELCOME TO THE *ASTROLOGY DIARY 2026*

As we embark on this journey through the celestial rhythms of 2026, we find ourselves on the edge of a profound transformation. The stars and planets, in their timeless dance, offer us a map to navigate the coming year full of opportunities for growth, renewal and enlightenment.

In this diary, you will discover astrological insights and guidance tailored to help you make the most of every cosmic shift. This year, I have added suggestions for integrating working with crystals and chakras into your routine. Each day, you'll find an overview of the main astrological events. And each month you'll be able to prepare for retrogrades and eclipses through personalized tips for harnessing their energy in your daily life.

The year 2026 will be one of significant change. For the first time in many years, we will have a total shift in the energy of all ten astrological planetary greats! You are invited to embrace new beginnings, release outdated patterns and step into your true potential.

A portal is opening so that you can enter this New Age, but first you must let go of what no longer serves you. Whether you are seeking clarity in your personal life, career or relationships, the wisdom of the stars can inspire your journey.

Let this diary serve as a companion, offering you insight, inspiration and a sense of connection with the greater cosmos. Open this diary every morning and write a few lines of whatever comes to mind to connect you with your unconscious, your dreams, your intuition and your guides.

Let the movements of the planets point you toward a year of growth and renewal in which every challenge becomes an opportunity for self-discovery and empowerment.

Here's to a transformative and enlightening 2026!

Ana Leo

ZODIACS

ARIES

TAURUS

GEMINI

CANCER

LEO

VIRGO

LIBRA

SCORPIO

SAGITTARIUS

CAPRICORN

AQUARIUS

PISCES

PLANETS & NODES

SUN

MOON

MERCURY

VENUS

MARS

JUPITER

SATURN

URANUS

NEPTUNE

PLUTO

NORTH NODE

SOUTH NODE

KIRON

ELEMENTS & ASPECTS

FIRE

EARTH

AIR

WATER

CONJUNCTION
0°

SQUARE
90°

SEXTILE
60°

TRINE
120°

OPPOSITION
180°

RETROGRADE   DIRECT   STATION

MY ASTRAL CHART

Go to astro.com and make your free chart. Copy the position of each planet into this chart. You're starting to get in touch with every aspect of your birth chart. Make a note of which sign each planet is in and the exact degrees. Then draw the symbols of the planets inside the wheel and write the signs for each house on the last line of the circle. Don't worry about the aspects or the lines that appear on the website – at this point just get in touch with the planetary positions.

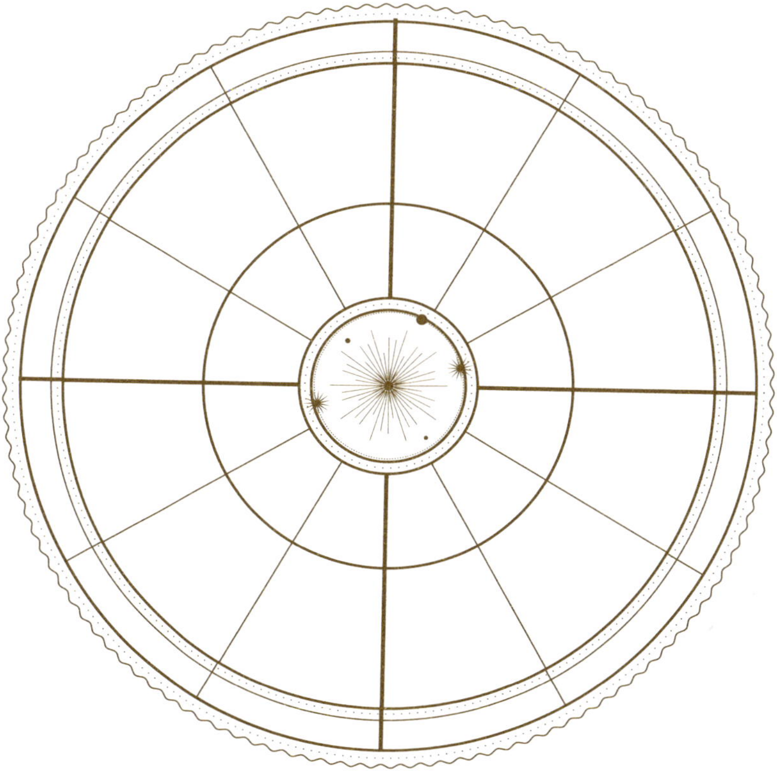

☉ _____

☽ _____

☿ _____

♀ _____

♂ _____

♃ _____

♄ _____

♅ _____

♆ _____

♇ _____

☊ _____

☋ _____

LUNAR CALENDAR

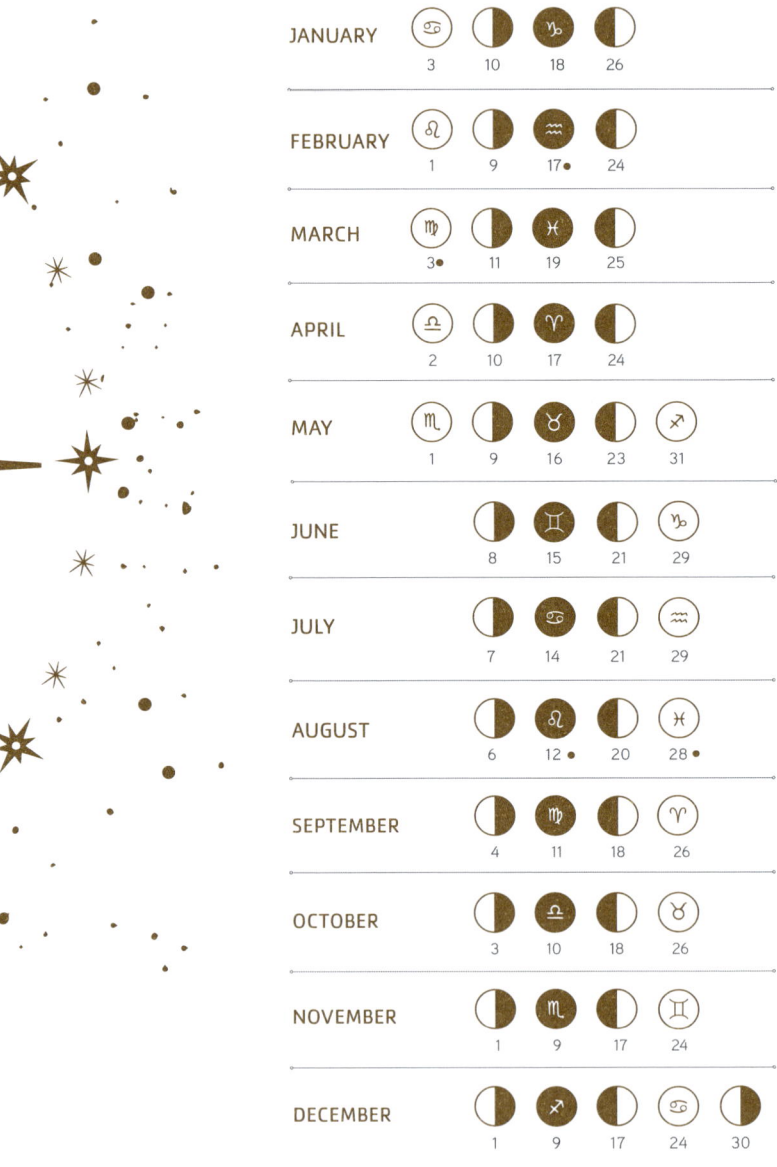

JANUARY	♋ 3	◐ 10	♑ 18	◑ 26	
FEBRUARY	♌ 1	◐ 9	♒ 17●	◑ 24	
MARCH	♍ 3●	◐ 11	♓ 19	◑ 25	
APRIL	♎ 2	◐ 10	♈ 17	◑ 24	
MAY	♏ 1	◐ 9	♉ 16	◑ 23	♐ 31
JUNE	◐ 8	♊ 15	◑ 21	♑ 29	
JULY	◐ 7	♋ 14	◑ 21	♒ 29	
AUGUST	◐ 6	♌ 12●	◑ 20	♓ 28●	
SEPTEMBER	◐ 4	♍ 11	◑ 18	♈ 26	
OCTOBER	◐ 3	♎ 10	◑ 18	♉ 26	
NOVEMBER	◐ 1	♏ 9	◑ 17	♊ 24	
DECEMBER	◐ 1	♐ 9	◑ 17	♋ 24	◐ 30

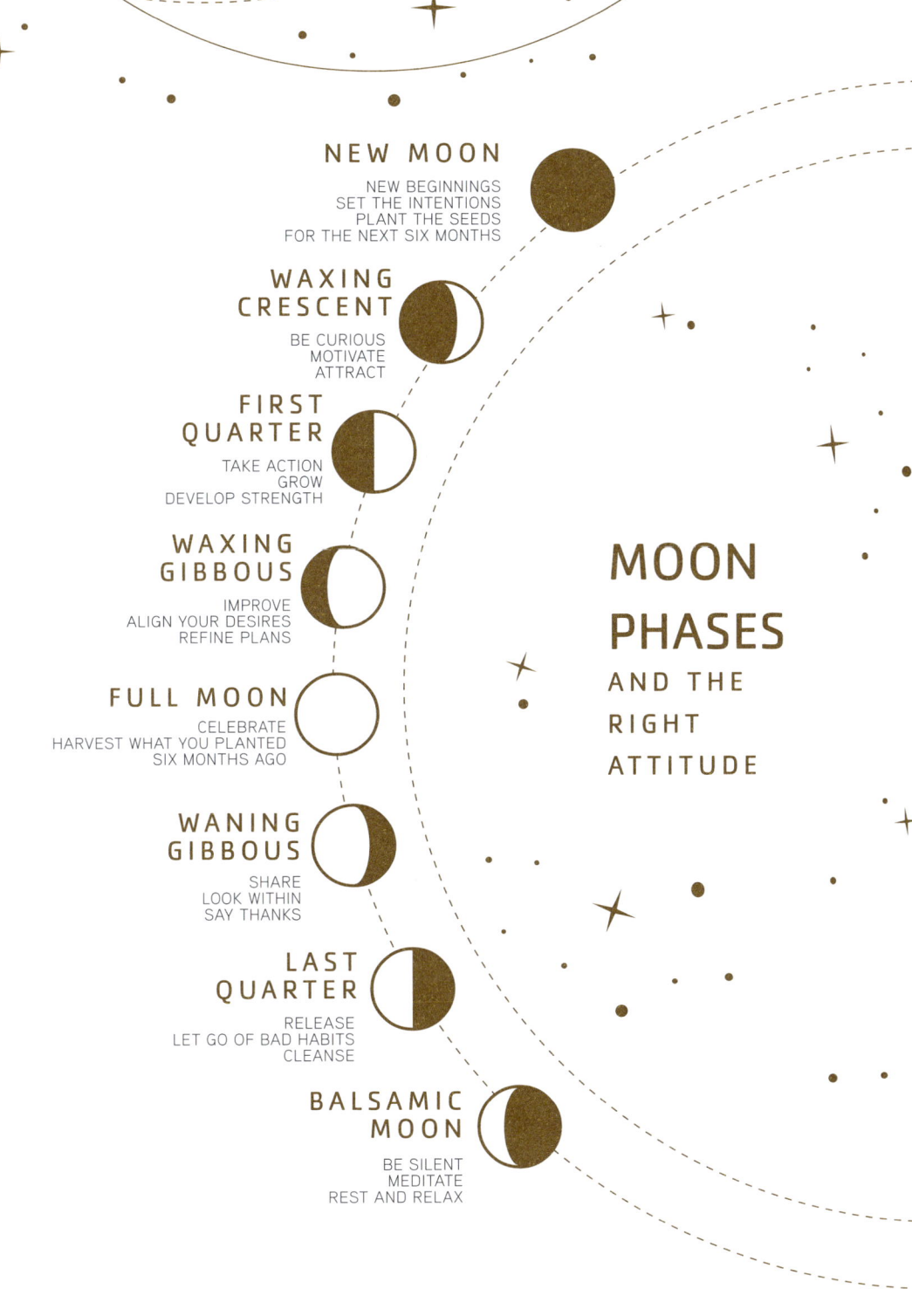

NEW MOON

NEW BEGINNINGS
SET THE INTENTIONS
PLANT THE SEEDS
FOR THE NEXT SIX MONTHS

**WAXING
CRESCENT**

BE CURIOUS
MOTIVATE
ATTRACT

**FIRST
QUARTER**

TAKE ACTION
GROW
DEVELOP STRENGTH

**WAXING
GIBBOUS**

IMPROVE
ALIGN YOUR DESIRES
REFINE PLANS

FULL MOON

CELEBRATE
HARVEST WHAT YOU PLANTED
SIX MONTHS AGO

**WANING
GIBBOUS**

SHARE
LOOK WITHIN
SAY THANKS

**LAST
QUARTER**

RELEASE
LET GO OF BAD HABITS
CLEANSE

**BALSAMIC
MOON**

BE SILENT
MEDITATE
REST AND RELAX

MOON
PHASES
AND THE
RIGHT
ATTITUDE

SOLAR CALENDAR

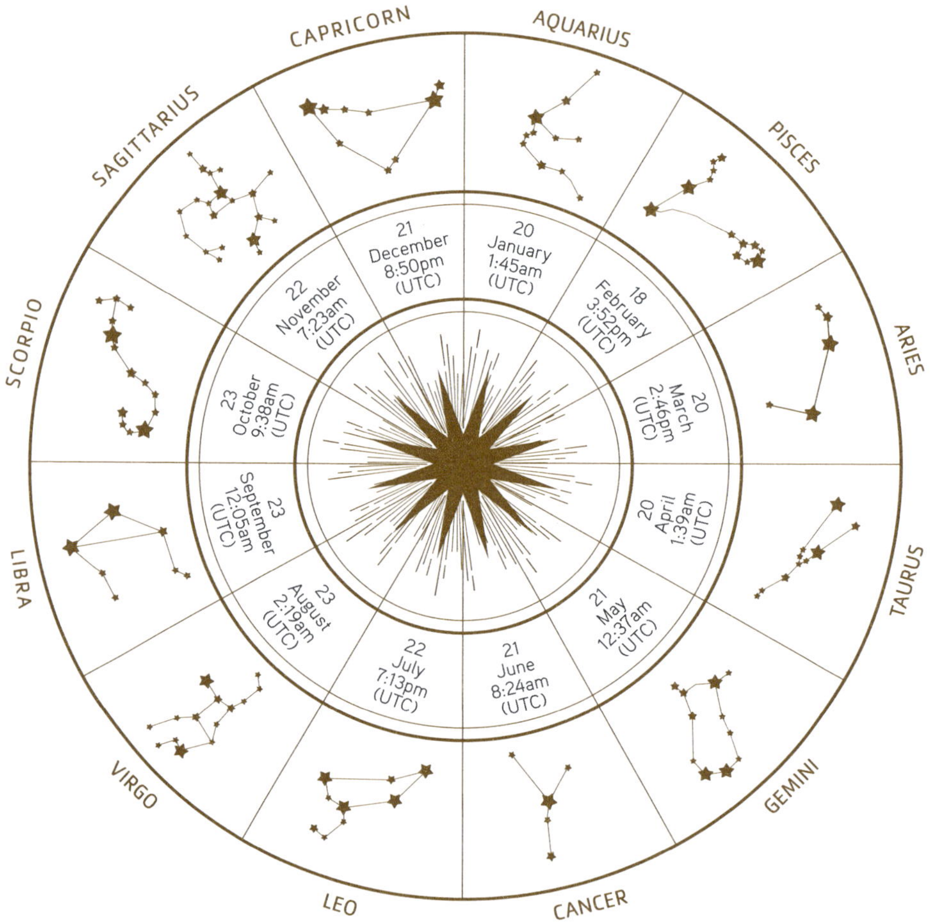

CAPRICORN

AQUARIUS

SAGITTARIUS

PISCES

SCORPIO

ARIES

21 December 8:50pm (UTC)

20 January 1:45am (UTC)

22 November 7:23am (UTC)

18 February 3:52pm (UTC)

23 October 9:38am (UTC)

20 March 2:46pm (UTC)

23 September 12:05am (UTC)

20 April 1:39am (UTC)

23 August 2:19am (UTC)

21 May 12:37am (UTC)

LIBRA

TAURUS

22 July 7:13pm (UTC)

21 June 8:24am (UTC)

VIRGO

GEMINI

LEO

CANCER

THE WHEEL OF THE YEAR

The below dates correlate to the Northern Hemisphere. You may need to change them to apply to the Southern Hemisphere.

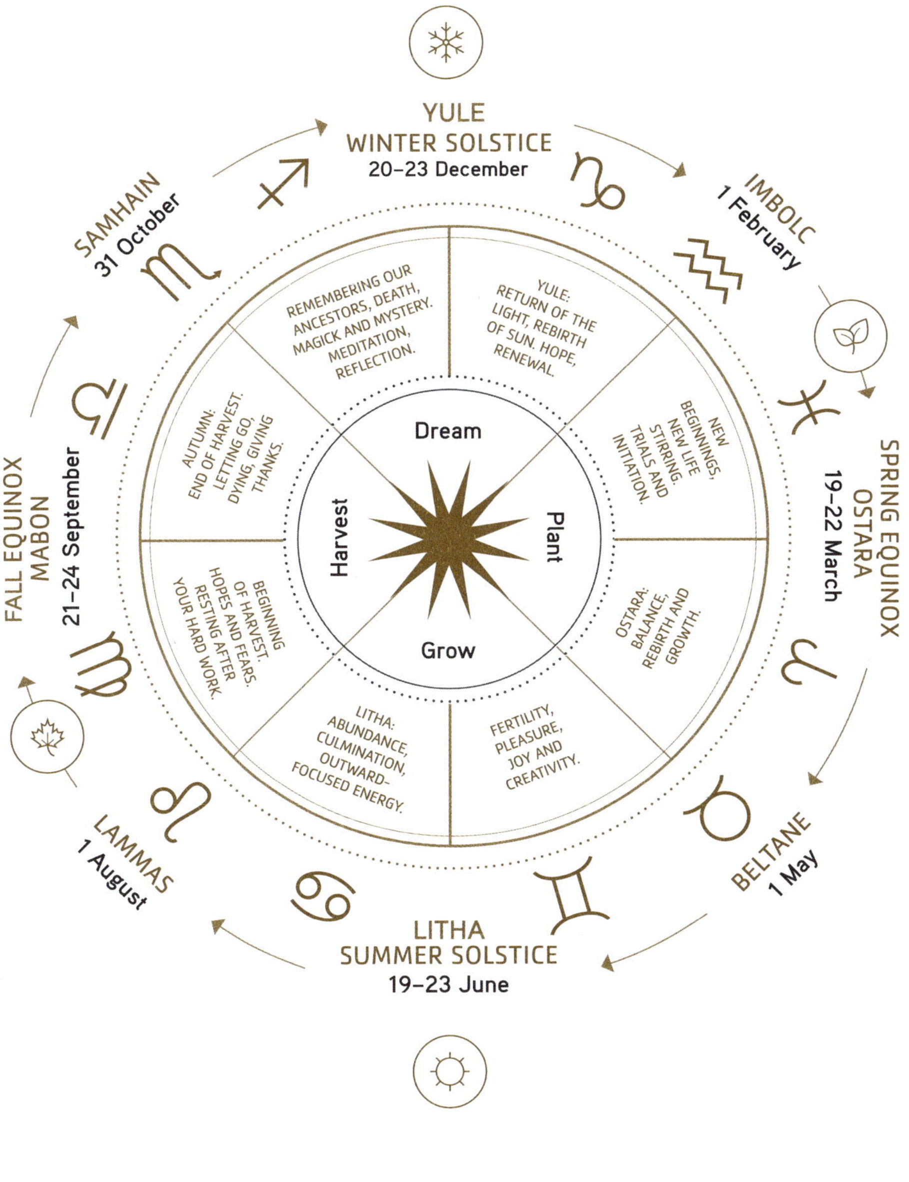

YULE
WINTER SOLSTICE
20–23 December

SAMHAIN
31 October

IMBOLC
1 February

FALL EQUINOX
MABON
21–24 September

SPRING EQUINOX
OSTARA
19–22 March

LAMMAS
1 August

BELTANE
1 May

LITHA
SUMMER SOLSTICE
19–23 June

Dream

Plant

Harvest

Grow

REMEMBERING OUR ANCESTORS, DEATH, MAGICK AND MYSTERY. MEDITATION, REFLECTION.

YULE: RETURN OF THE LIGHT, REBIRTH OF SUN. HOPE, RENEWAL.

AUTUMN: END OF HARVEST. LETTING GO, DYING, GIVING THANKS.

NEW BEGINNINGS, NEW LIFE, STIRRING, TRIALS AND INITIATION.

BEGINNING OF HARVEST. HOPES AND FEARS. RESTING AFTER YOUR HARD WORK.

OSTARA: BALANCE, REBIRTH AND GROWTH.

LITHA: ABUNDANCE, CULMINATION, OUTWARD-FOCUSED ENERGY.

FERTILITY, PLEASURE, JOY AND CREATIVITY.

RETROGRADE PLANETS

MERCURY
26 FEB–20 MAR / 22° ♓–8° ♓
29 JUN–23 JUL / 26° ♋–16° ♋
24 OCT–13 NOV / 21° ♏–5° ♏

VENUS
3 OCT–13 NOV / 8° ♏–23° ♎

MARS
NO RETROGRADITY THIS YEAR

JUPITER
11 NOV 25–11 MAR 26 / 25° ♋–15° ♋
13 DEC 26–13 APR 27 / 27° ♌–17° ♌

SATURN
27 JUL–10 DEC / 14° ♈–8° ♈

URANUS
6 SEP 25–4 FEB 26 / 1° ♊–27° ♉
10 SEP 26–8 FEB 27 / 5° ♊–1° ♊

NEPTUNE
7 JUL–12 DEC / 4° ♈–2° ♈

PLUTO
7 MAY–16 OCT / 5° ♒–3° ♒

WHAT IS THE NEW MOON?

Every month, the Sun and Moon meet in the sky. This meeting is undoubtedly the most powerful moment in the entire lunar cycle as it contains the perfect energy to start a new chapter.

During the New Moon, the Sun and Moon are in the same mathematical degree in the Zodiac. Together they join forces to help us work for our intentions. It is this unity that creates a powerful vibration in the Universe and within each one of us. Our strength and emotion are together, as if an energetic and cosmic portal has been opened, and we are invited to sow a seed of what we need to manifest in our lives. So the New Moon is the perfect time to take a first step or start a project because the energy of the Moon is so strong that we can direct it to make great energetic leaps in our lives.

At the Full Moon we observe our entire journey in the last six months. It is the culmination of the events that emerged at the New Moon. It is when the Sun is on the opposite side of the Moon, illuminating her conquests and opposing her energy. Use the two weeks after the New Moon to walk toward your goal and observe the first steps of your intentions. Work hand in hand with these cycles, so that in six months' time, when the Full Moon finally happens in that same sign, you will have manifested a new reality in your life.

Besides giving us the opportunity to start something, the New Moon also allows us an opening to balance our entire internal being: our soul, mind and spirit. Through the union of the Sun and the Moon, every month we have a new opportunity to create balance in our internal and external energies and, consequently, in our lives.

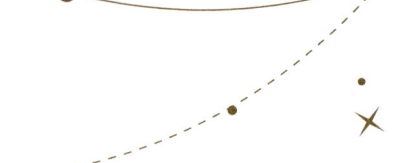

HOW TO MAKE THE MOST OF THIS MOMENT

When the Sun and Moon are balanced, so are we. Each month, this diary will show you the ideal "theme" to work on, both in terms of your feelings and your actions.

The house on the astral chart, where the New Moon takes place, gives us clues, showing us the area of our life where we must put all our intentions in motion.

The New Moon pages in this diary were created to guide you in the use of these energies and to help you identify the areas to be worked on. In some months you will be more motivated to act; in others, you will be helped to vibrate what you want to feel.

Through the lens of the Zodiac, we are able to identify the right time to take action to transform our reality. The balance of these two vital energies is the key. When the two celestial bodies – the two most important luminaries for our daily life – come together in the sky to balance their energies, we must balance ours too.

HOW TO MANIFEST

The exact moment of the New Moon possesses the greatest energetic force, so it is a time when you can plant your intentions for the next cycle.

The 12 hours before this event are charged with this energy and must be used, both for introspection and for reflection. Six months separate a New Moon from a Full Moon, in the same sign.

This is the period when we see our desire grow. Following its development, it is time to take care of it and give it the necessary attention so that it manifests itself. Remember that your desire is like a seed that needs to be nourished every day, so that it grows and bears flowers and fruits. Just creating the list and not taking any action to make it a reality will not lift it off the paper.

Put at least five intentions on your list, always pointing out the necessary action for it to become reality. For example: I intend to lose 5kg (11lb) – I will start walking three times a week. I intend to get a job – I will rewrite my resumé and send it to a specific company I want to work for.

Make sure that you are asking from your soul, not your ego. The soul's desires require patience and dedication, and bring you long-term satisfaction. The ego's desires are superficial and only benefit you; your satisfaction is immediate and does not last for long.

Remember that you must feel as if you are already fulfilling all your wishes, so when you write them, imagine yourself as if they were already a reality. How would you feel? What would you say to other people? How would you describe it to the person who most wants to see your success? The greater the detail in your imagination, the better.

WHICH TIME ZONE IS CONSIDERED?

Adjust Coordinated Universal Time (UTC) times to your time zone, which is provided on the New Moon pages.

PST – Pacific Standard Time or PDT – Pacific Daylight Time
CST – Central Standard Time or CDT – Central Daylight Time
EST – Eastern Standard Time or EDT – Eastern Daylight Time
GMT – Greenwich Mean Time or IST/BST – Irish/British Summer Time
CET – Central European Time or CEST – Central European Summer Time
AEST – Australian Eastern Standard Time or AEDT – Australian Eastern
    Daylight Time

All the information in this diary has the intention of alerting you before the aspect reaches its apex. As they are at least eight hours ahead of the Pacific, European countries should consider the day to start at 8:00am. So if the exact aspect perfection occurs before then, the advice will be posted one day before. Most US readers should consider the day to start between 12:00am and 3:00pm as usual. An aspect is always strongest as it builds, and then gradually weakens after it reaches its perfection (same degree and minute). Australian and Asian residents can prepare one day earlier. No matter where you are, with this diary, you will always be ready for the best energy to come!

THE 12 HOUSES
OF THE HOROSCOPE

I. FIRST HOUSE: Personality, natural disposition, worldly outlook generally. Physical experiences as obtained through the five senses. The parts of the body denoted are the head and face.

II. SECOND HOUSE: Finance, monetary prospects, self-esteem, salary. Desires caused by the influence of the tenth house affect moral growth. The parts of the body denoted are the throat and ears.

III. THIRD HOUSE: Relatives and kin, travelling, intellect, first education, expression and minor impressions made upon the physical brain. The parts of the body denoted are the neck, arms and shoulders and lungs.

IV. FOURTH HOUSE: Hereditary tendencies, home and domestic life, ancestry, environment and the general state of things at the close of life. The parts of the body denoted are the breasts, stomach and digestive organs.

V. FIFTH HOUSE: Offspring, generative powers, sensations, worldly enterprise and energy. Creativity and talents. The parts of the body denoted are the loins, heart and back.

VI. SIXTH HOUSE: Service and attachments arising from the expression of the tenth house. This house denotes sickness arising from worry and anxiety. It is also the house of phenomenal magick arising from everyday habits. The parts of the body denoted are the bowels and solar plexus.

VII. SEVENTH HOUSE: Union, marriage, business partner, individual character, your client, your other half. The parts of the body denoted are the veins and kidneys.

VIII. EIGHTH HOUSE: The womb, pregnancy, gestation, fusion of energies, sexual drive, death and all matters pertaining to legacies or affairs connected with death. The parts of the body denoted are the secret parts and the generative system.

IX. NINTH HOUSE: Higher mentality, higher studies, science, philosophy and religion, the searching of the path, truth, long journeys, dreams and image-making power. The parts of the body denoted are the thighs and hips.

X. TENTH HOUSE: Profession, business, fame, honour and material reputation. All worldly activities and moral responsibilities are shown by this house to succeed. The parts of the body denoted are the knees.

XI. ELEVENTH HOUSE: Hopes, wishes, aspiration, friends, acquaintances, social groups, audience and followers. The parts of the body denoted are the legs and ankles.

XII. TWELFTH HOUSE: Occult tendencies. Its connection with the fourth house shows the psychic thought inheritance from the past, and the result is either joy or sorrow. This may be said to be the most critical house of the 12. The parts of the body denoted are the feet and toes.

LIFE SATISFACTION CHART

Each section represents an area of your life, or a house in your astral chart.
On a scale from 1 to 10, rate the areas of your chart.
You can use colour pencils to make it artistic.

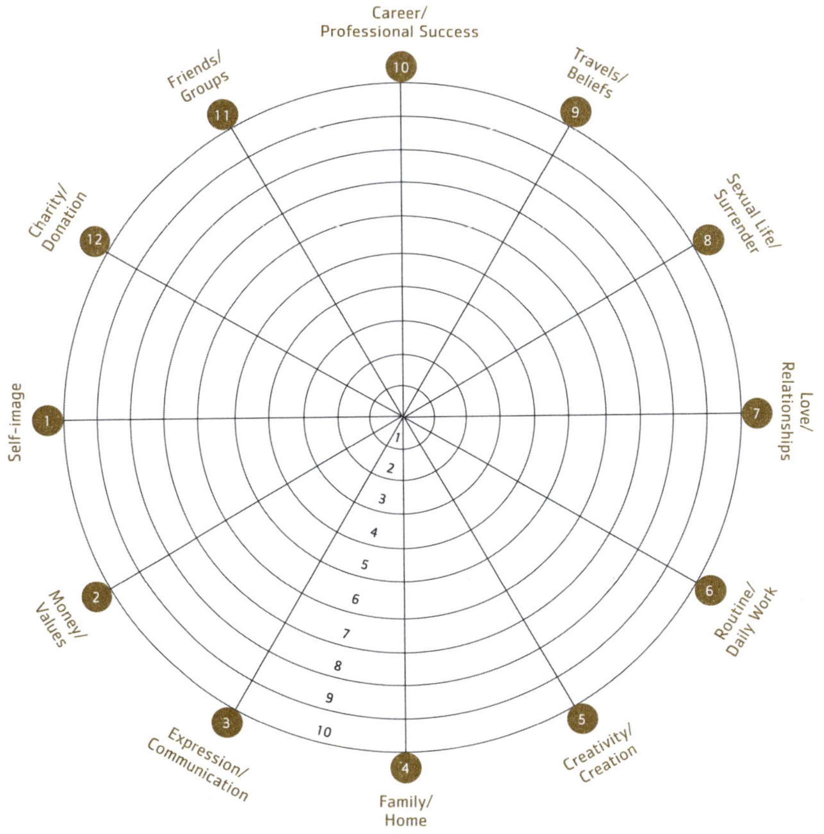

Career/
Professional Success

Friends/
Groups

Travels/
Beliefs

Charity/
Donation

Sexual Life/
Surrender

Self-image

Love/
Relationships

Money/
Values

Routine/
Daily Work

Expression/
Communication

Creativity/
Creation

Family/
Home

10   11   12   1   2   3   4   5   6   7   8   9

1   2   3   4   5   6   7   8   9   10

What could you do to increase your level of satisfaction in the areas
you have scored the lowest? Which is the area of your life that, when
you are satisfied, can improve all the other areas? Take time to think
about it and always come back to this page to track your progress.

TAROT & ASTROLOGY

0. THE FOOL		AIR/URANUS	New beginnings, wonder, innocence, foolishness
1. THE MAGICIAN		MERCURY	Mastery, creation, willpower, manifestation
2. THE HIGH PRIESTESS		MOON	Intuition, divine wisdom, inner voice
3. THE EMPRESS		VENUS	Creativity, beauty, nurturing, fertility
4. THE EMPEROR		ARIES	Authority, ambition, fostering discipline
5. THE HIEROPHANT		TAURUS	Tradition, convention, spiritual wisdom
6. THE LOVERS		GEMINI	Love, union, relationship choices
7. THE CHARIOT		CANCER	Discipline, self-control, success
8. STRENGTH		LEO	Courage, inner strength, compassion
9. THE HERMIT		VIRGO	Insight, awareness, solitude, contemplation
10. WHEEL OF FORTUNE		JUPITER	Destiny, karma, fate, fortune

11. JUSTICE		LIBRA	Truth, law, fairness, cause and effect, clarity
12. THE HANGED MAN		WATER/NEPTUNE	Sacrifice, release, new perspective
13. DEATH		SCORPIO	Change, transformation, end of cycle
14. TEMPERANCE		SAGITTARIUS	Patience, finding meaning, balance
15. THE DEVIL		CAPRICORN	Materialism, pleasure, obsession, addiction
16. THE TOWER		MARS	Foundational shift, upheaval, drastic change
17. THE STAR		AQUARIUS	Faith, hope, healing, rejuvenation
18. THE MOON		PISCES	Intuition, unconsciousness, illusions
19. THE SUN		SUN	Joy, success, pleasure, celebration
20. JUDGEMENT		FIRE/PLUTO	Reflection, awakening, reckoning
21. THE WORLD		EARTH/SATURN	Completion, peace, fulfilment, harmony

A SPELL FOR EACH
TIME AND EACH SIGN

Combine the energy of your sign or the sign in transit at every
moment to improve your magical abilities even more.

♈ **Fire Witch** – Focuses on the fire element, does a lot of work involving candles, burning, etc.

♉ **Green Witch** – Focused on the use of herbs and plants in magick, very natural and Earth-based.

♊ **Crystal Witch** – Works with stones, crystals, gemstones, for healing and other spells, deals with chakras.

♋ **Kitchen Witch** – Uses magick incorporated into cooking and baking. Can conjure items for spells or ritual use.

♌ **Lunar Witch** – Attunes to/honours the Moon cycles and phases. Likes to wake at night under the Moon energy.

♍ **Forest Witch** – Works best surrounded by trees, is familiar with local plants and animals and herbal healing.

♎ **Music Witch** – Its magick is deeply rooted in music, has a certain connection with sound and uses that to enhance rituals.

♏ **Nocturnal Witch** – Embraces darker energies, likes night-time and its mysteries. Works mostly after midnight.

♐ **Storm Witch** – Combines its energy with that of the weather. Collects elements such as rainwater, leaves and rocks for spells.

♑ **Astronomy Witch** – All its magick aligns with stars and planets. Practises astrology, recognizes placements and their significance.

♒ **Divination Witch** – Works with various forms of divination, such as tarot reading, palmistry, tea leaves, geomancy.

♓ **Sea Witch** – Uses oceans and their magick practices, utilizing the natural objects in the sea such as salt water, shells and driftwood.

SACRED ALTAR

A simple ritual for creating a sacred space is to arrange the elements according to the cardinal directions. The left side has Yin energy, while the right side carries the Yang polarity. Invoke the guardian elements to help you create your own magick. When you have finished your ritual, remember to close the circle, thanking the spirits and saying goodbye to them.

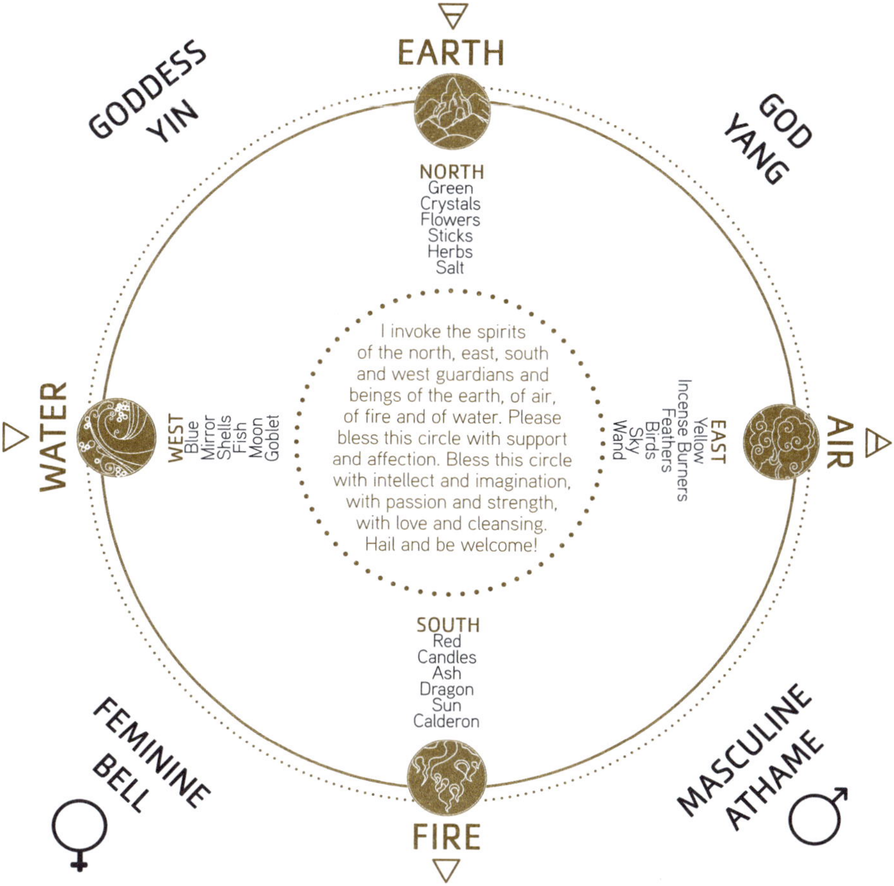

GODDESS YIN

GOD YANG

EARTH ▽

NORTH
Green
Crystals
Flowers
Sticks
Herbs
Salt

WATER ▷

WEST
Blue
Mirror
Shells
Fish
Moon
Goblet

AIR ▷

EAST
Yellow
Incense Burners
Feathers
Birds
Sky
Wand

I invoke the spirits of the north, east, south and west guardians and beings of the earth, of air, of fire and of water. Please bless this circle with support and affection. Bless this circle with intellect and imagination, with passion and strength, with love and cleansing. Hail and be welcome!

SOUTH
Red
Candles
Ash
Dragon
Sun
Calderon

FEMININE BELL ♀

MASCULINE ATHAME ♂

FIRE ▽

CRYSTALOSCOPIA

Activate the four elements of your birth chart with crystals

Select a particular crystal to connect with during each sign and find out its element. Choose your crystal according to how well it resonates with you – there's no need to overthink it! It is your interaction with the stone that will enhance the attunement.

First, connect genuinely and directly with your crystal before seeking out extra information about the stone, so you don't have any prior expectations. Your interaction is unique and any messages you receive from the crystal are for you at that moment. This is an opportunity to increase your confidence in your intuition.

Establish your practice and use this diary to explore connections between the crystals you use and events and movements in the sky. Over time, you'll be able to spot and analyse certain patterns and build up your own catalogue of crystals.

SOME SUGGESTIONS

To cleanse your energy quickly and safety, place your crystals on a druse (a crystal formation) or selenite. Sound is also a great option – try using tuning forks, sound bowls or even your own voice.

To connect, lie down with the crystal positioned intuitively on your body, or simply hold it during meditation. If you are familiar with the chakras, you can place your crystal in the chosen chakra centre. Visualize the crystal expanding so that you can enter it and get involved in its energy. The secret is to connect frequently so that you can integrate crystal magick into your daily routine.

If you enjoy performing rituals, incorporate the use of crystals and sacred geometry into them. If you only have one stone, place it in the centre; if you have more, form patterns and mandalas with them to anchor energy or open portals.

FIRE CRYSTALS Yellow calcite, orange calcite, tiger's eye, pyrite

EARTH CRYSTALS Hematite, red jasper, green quartz, black tourmaline

AIR CRYSTALS Angelite, fluorite, fuchsite, sodalite

WATER CRYSTALS Amazonite, emerald, lepidolite, pink tourmaline

May you receive lots of insight, an expansion of consciousness and a multitude of crystalline blessings!

By Jana Tahira @YNNA.space
Creator Cristaloscopia.com

IMPORTANT NOTE: Use crystals responsibly and with awareness, aligning your practice with caring for the planet. You are nature. Soon we will access this energy only etherically.

FLOWER OF LIFE

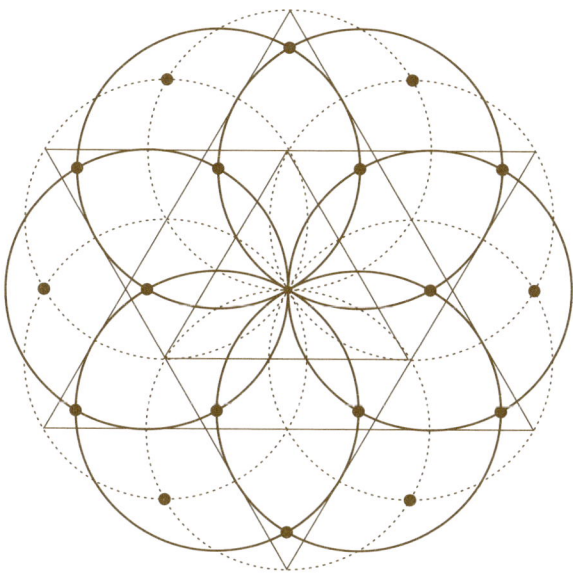

I first came across the Flower of Life diagram at university. I was amazed at how six circles could begin to form such a delicate and organic figure. This geometric symbol, which consists of a series of overlapping circles arranged to form a flower or rosette, stayed with me for years, until I realized what it meant through astrology.

The Flower of Life diagram has ancient roots and is found in various cultures around the world. It is often associated with spiritual and metaphysical meanings. Some people believe that the Flower of Life pattern represents the creation of the Universe and the sacred geometry that permeates our entire existence.

If we use this graphic in spiritual practices, meditation and in studies of geometry, we can reach even higher levels of consciousness. It is believed that this ancient symbol contains profound information and energies and that meditating on it or using it in some way can lead to spiritual insights and harmony.

MEDITATION TIPS

Use the nodes in this figure to represent the astrological houses in your birth chart. Place crystals on each of the points, activating the energy of each area of your life.

Using a compass, redraw the Flower of Life on top of your birth chart. See which area falls within the sacred geometry pattern.

You can colour, paint and draw on the mandala. Draw new shapes, connect the points already highlighted or create new ones.

CHAKRAS

The energy centres of the body, also known as the chakras, form an intrinsic part of various spiritual traditions and belief systems, including Hinduism, Tibetan Buddhism and the energy healing system of reiki. There is an association between the chakras and the endocrine glands of the body. This connection is often seen as a way of understanding how the chakras can influence the physical and emotional functioning of the human body. The idea is that each chakra is linked to a specific endocrine gland, which in turn influences different aspects of health and wellbeing.

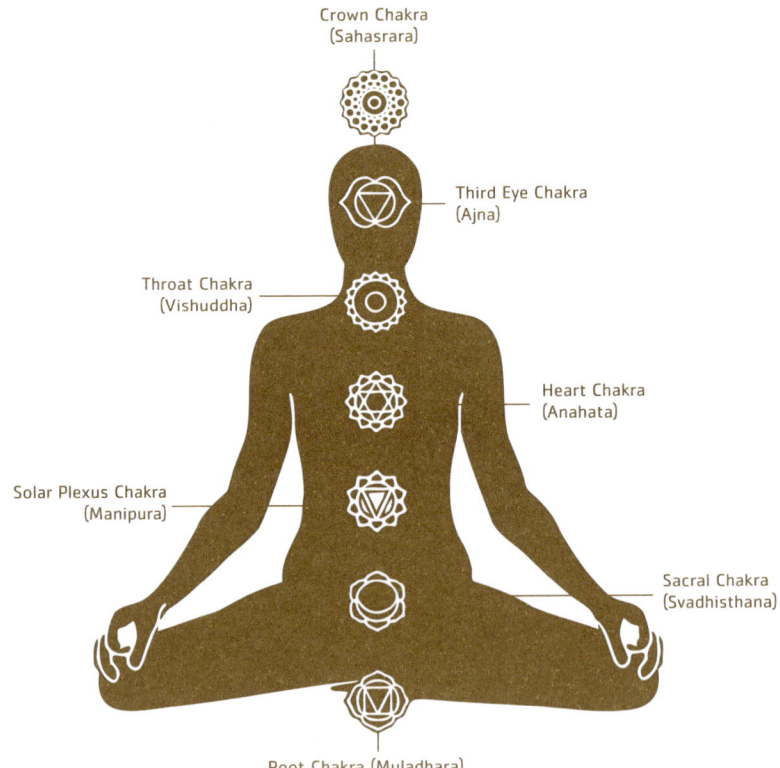

Crown Chakra
(Sahasrara)

Third Eye Chakra
(Ajna)

Throat Chakra
(Vishuddha)

Heart Chakra
(Anahata)

Solar Plexus Chakra
(Manipura)

Sacral Chakra
(Svadhisthana)

Root Chakra (Muladhara)

Here are some of the common associations between chakras and endocrine glands:

 THE CROWN CHAKRA (SAHASRARA): This chakra is found at the top of the head and is associated with the pineal and pituitary glands, depending on the tradition. It signifies spirituality, a connection with the divine and higher consciousness. Its colour is violet or white.

 THE THIRD EYE CHAKRA (AJNA): Located in the centre of the forehead between the eyebrows, this chakra is linked with the pineal gland, which plays a role in intuition and regulating our circadian rhythms. It is related to inner perception and wisdom, and its colour is indigo or dark blue.

 THE THROAT CHAKRA (VISHUDDHA): This chakra is found in the throat and is associated with the thyroid gland, which regulates metabolism and communication. It is linked to verbal expression and truth, and its colour is light blue.

 THE HEART CHAKRA (ANAHATA): Located in the centre of the chest, this chakra is connected to the thymus, which helps to regulate the immune system. It is related to love, compassion, emotional harmony and our connections with others. Its colour is green or pink.

 THE SOLAR PLEXUS CHAKRA (MANIPURA): Found in the area of the solar plexus, this chakra is connected with the pancreas. It is associated with personal power, self-esteem, digestion and confidence. Its colour is yellow.

 THE SACRAL CHAKRA (SVADHISTHANA): This chakra is located in the lower abdomen and is related to the reproductive organs and the ovaries in women and the testicles in men. It is connected with sexuality, creativity, the emotions and pleasure. Its colour is orange.

 THE ROOT CHAKRA (MULADHARA): Found at the base of the spine or in the perineum, it is associated with the adrenal glands. It is linked to survival, security, stability, vital energy and the stress response – our basic needs. Its colour is red.

When these chakras are balanced and working correctly, we experience a state of good physical and emotional health, as well as spiritual balance. However, imbalances in the chakras can lead to physical, emotional or spiritual problems. Practices such as meditation, yoga, reiki and other energy therapies are useful tools to balance the chakras and promote wellbeing.

THE
DEFINITIVE GUIDE
TO SELF-CARE

FOR THE MIND

- Go offline on your social media
- Listen to your favourite music
- Have a bite of something sweet
- Do something creative
- Fix something broken in your house
- Bake a cake or biscuits
- Clean out your wardrobe and donate your clothes
- Watch your favourite film or series
- Take 15 minutes to meditate
- Declutter your space
- Create a praise pot
- Organize your drawers
- Read a new book
- Prepare a home-cooked meal
- Listen to your favourite podcast
- Drink tea in a nice cup
- Buy yourself some flowers
- Organize your desktop files

FOR THE BODY

- Wear your favourite clothes
- Stay outside in the Sun for 15 minutes
- Be still, practise silence
- Light your favourite candle
- Encourage yourself to laugh
- Take a nap if you need to
- Practise breath work
- Run or walk for 30 minutes
- Dance like a child
- Stretch for 20 minutes
- Make a healthier lunch choice
- Take a class, learn something new
- In cold weather, wrap yourself in a soft blanket

FOR THE SOUL

- Help someone
- Write down your thoughts
- Go on a date with yourself
- Listen to your emotions
- Spend time with loved ones
- Play with a pet
- Splurge on something you really want
- Reward yourself by practising a hobby
- Hug someone
- Stay home for two days
- Enjoy a home spa
- Call a friend to arrange lunch
- Plan a quick trip to nature
- Spend time alone
- Write a love letter to yourself
- Make a list of things to be grateful for
- Make a visual board of your future
- Draw a map of all the places you've ever been
- Make a list of dreams
- Cry if you want to
- Go to a bookstore or library
- Look at old photos and videos from the past
- Read poetry
- Make a list of long- and medium-term goals
- Admire yourself in the mirror

JANUARY

M	T	W	T	F	S	S
			1	2	**3**	**4**
5	6	7	8	9	**10**	11
12	13	14	15	16	**17**	18
19	20	21	22	23	**24**	25
26	27	28	29	30	**31**	

FEBRUARY

M	T	W	T	F	S	S
						1
2	3	4	5	6	**7**	**8**
9	10	11	12	13	**14**	**15**
16	17	18	19	20	**21**	**22**
23	24	25	26	27	**28**	

MARCH

M	T	W	T	F	S	S
						1
2	3	4	5	6	**7**	**8**
9	10	11	12	13	**14**	**15**
16	17	18	19	20	**21**	**22**
23	24	25	26	27	**28**	**29**
30	31					

APRIL

M	T	W	T	F	S	S
	1	2	3	**4**	**5**	
6	7	8	9	10	**11**	**12**
13	14	15	16	17	**18**	**19**
20	21	22	23	24	**25**	**26**
27	28	29	30			

MAY

M	T	W	T	F	S	S
				1	**2**	**3**
4	5	6	7	8	**9**	**10**
11	12	13	14	15	**16**	**17**
18	19	20	21	22	**23**	**24**
25	26	27	28	29	**30**	**31**

JUNE

M	T	W	T	F	S	S
1	2	3	4	5	**6**	**7**
8	9	10	11	12	**13**	**14**
15	16	17	18	19	**20**	**21**
22	23	24	25	26	**27**	**28**
29	30					

JULY

M	T	W	T	F	S	S
	1	2	3	**4**	**5**	
6	7	8	9	10	**11**	**12**
13	14	15	16	17	**18**	**19**
20	21	22	23	24	**25**	**26**
27	28	29	30	31		

AUGUST

M	T	W	T	F	S	S
					1	**2**
3	4	5	6	7	**8**	**9**
10	11	12	13	14	**15**	**16**
17	18	19	20	21	**22**	**23**
24	25	26	27	28	**29**	**30**
31						

SEPTEMBER

M	T	W	T	F	S	S
	1	2	3	4	**5**	**6**
7	8	9	10	11	**12**	**13**
14	15	16	17	18	**19**	**20**
21	22	23	24	25	**26**	**27**
28	29	30				

OCTOBER

M	T	W	T	F	S	S
			1	2	**3**	**4**
5	6	7	8	9	**10**	11
12	13	14	15	16	**17**	18
19	20	21	22	23	**24**	25
26	27	28	29	30	**31**	

NOVEMBER

M	T	W	T	F	S	S
						1
2	3	4	5	6	**7**	**8**
9	10	11	12	13	**14**	**15**
16	17	18	19	20	**21**	**22**
23	24	25	26	27	**28**	**29**
30						

DECEMBER

M	T	W	T	F	S	S
	1	2	3	4	**5**	**6**
7	8	9	10	11	**12**	**13**
14	15	16	17	18	**19**	**20**
21	22	23	24	25	**26**	**27**
28	29	30	31			

01	JAN	New Year's Day	21	JUN	Father's Day
14	FEB	Valentine's Day	21	JUN	Summer Solstice
15	MAR	Mother's Day (UK)	31	AUG	Summer Bank Holiday (UK)
20	MAR	Spring Equinox	23	SEP	Autumn Equinox
03	APR	Good Friday	31	OCT	Halloween
05	APR	Easter Sunday	26	NOV	Thanksgiving
06	APR	Easter Monday	21	DEC	Winter Solstice
04	MAY	Early May Bank Holiday (UK)	25	DEC	Christmas Day
10	MAY	Mother's Day (USA)	26	DEC	Boxing Day
25	MAY	Spring Bank Holiday (UK)	31	DEC	New Year's Eve

MON	TUE	WED
05	06	07
12	13	14
19	20	21
	☉ ♒	
26	27	28
◑ ♉		

JANUARY

The following are the planetary changes that will happen this month

MERCURY

MOVES TO ♑ 1 JAN

MOVES TO ♒ 20 JAN

VENUS

MOVES TO ♒ 17 JAN

SUN

MOVES TO ♒ 20 JAN

MARS

MOVES TO ♒ 23 JAN

NEPTUNE

MOVES TO ♈ 23 JAN

THU	FRI	SAT	SUN
01	02	03 ○ ♋	04
08	09	10 ◐ ♎	11
15	16	17	18 ● ♑
22	23	24	25
29	30	31	

DEC
31
WED

☽ ♊
Moon in Gemini

JAN
01
THU

☿ ♐ □ ♆ ♓
Mercury in Sagittarius squares Neptune in Pisces

Welcome to 2026! This is an excellent aspect that helps us daydream and imagine a world without borders, where love will always rule. Think about your aspirations for this next chapter.

☿ ♑
Mercury enters Capricorn until 20 January

After dreaming big, Mercury enters Capricorn, advising you to write down your desires and start planning. Get to work!

☽ ♊
Moon in Gemini

JAN
02
FRI

☉ ♑ ✱ ☊ ♓
Sun in Capricorn sextile North Node in Pisces

This is an excellent opportunity to combine your worldly ambition with your spiritual vision. Think about how to balance these two aspects today.

☽ ♋
Moon in Cancer

JAN
03
SAT

♀ ♑ ✱ ☊ ♓
Venus in Capricorn sextile North Node in Pisces

Now it's time for Venus to combine her values with her holistic view of the world. How do you balance the material and the spiritual?

○ ♋
Full Moon 13º in Cancer at 10:03am (UTC)

First Full Moon of the year, reminding us to always surround ourselves with those who nurture us emotionally. Make dinner for the ones you love!

T	F	S	S	M	T	W	T	F	S	S	M	T	W	T	F	S	S	M	T	W	T	F	S	S	M	T	W	T	F	S
1	2	3	4	5	6	7	8	9	10	11	12	13	14	15	16	17	18	19	20	21	22	23	24	25	26	27	28	29	30	31

JAN
04
SUN

☽ ♌
Moon in Leo

JAN
05
MON

☽ ♌
Moon in Leo

T F **S S** M T W T F **S S** M T W T F **S S** M T W T F **S S** M T W T F **S**
1 2 **3 4** 5 6 7 8 **9 10 11** 12 13 14 15 16 **17 18** 19 20 21 22 23 **24 25** 26 27 28 29 30 **31**

JAN

06

TUE

☉ ☌ ♀ ♑
Sun meets Venus in Capricorn

Enjoy the good things in life, but always beware of
overindulgence. In relationships, it will take a very special
person to help you reach your dreams. Be realistic!

☽ ♍
Moon in Virgo

JAN

07

WED

☽ ♍
Moon in Virgo

JAN
08
THU

♀ ☌ ♂ ♑
Venus meets Mars in Capricorn

The meeting of this cosmic couple brings
the possibility of partnerships that share your
values. Talk about the future with your partner.

☽ ♍
Moon in Virgo

JAN
09
FRI

☉ ☌ ♂ ♑
Sun meets Mars in Capricorn

Put your high ideals into practice in life and relationships.
It's a great Friday to work on building your future.

♀ ♑ ☍ ♃ ℞ ♋
Venus in Capricorn opposite Jupiter
Retrograde in Cancer

You have set high standards for love and relationships,
but Jupiter signals a need for care and affection. Try
to find a balance that makes you feel safe and cosy.

☿ ♑ ⚹ ☊ ♓
Mercury in Capricorn sextile North Node in Pisces

An eventful Friday ends with some insights
into how your holistic view of the world can be
manifested in your life. Be open to divine clues!

☽ ♎
Moon in Libra

T	F	S	S	M	T	W	T	F	S	S	M	T	W	T	F	S	S	M	T	W	T	F	S	S	M	T	W	T	F	S
1	2	3	4	5	6	7	8	9	10	11	12	13	14	15	16	17	18	19	20	21	22	23	24	25	26	27	28	29	30	31

JAN

10

SAT

☉ ♑ ☍ ♃ ℞ ♋
Sun in Capricorn opposite Jupiter Retrograde in Cancer

Now is the time for the Sun to assess how
aligned your professional life and career goals
are with your personal life and affections.

♂ ♑ ☍ ♃ ℞ ♋
Mars in Capricorn opposite Jupiter Retrograde in Cancer

Even though there's a lot to be done, Mars is
ready to help you slow down a bit, without
making you feel like you're procrastinating or
wasting time on sentimentality. You can do it!

◐ ♎
Last Quarter 20º in Libra at 3:48pm (UTC)

Let go of your desire to make everything look
perfect. We are always evolving, so allow yourself
to be imperfect in your emotional interactions.

JAN

11

SUN

☽ ♏
Moon in Scorpio

T F S S M T W T F S S M T W T F S S M T W T F S S M T W T F S
1 2 3 4 5 6 7 8 9 10 11 12 13 14 15 16 17 18 19 20 21 22 23 24 25 26 27 28 29 30 31

JAN
12
MON

☽ ♏
Moon in Scorpio

JAN
13
TUE

☽ ♐
Moon in Sagittarius

JAN

14

WED

♀ ♑ ☌ ♃ ℞ ♋
Mercury in Capricorn opposite Jupiter Retrograde in Cancer

Your mental health could be at risk in this aspect.
You feel you always have to be in charge, even when
you're the one who needs a little extra support. Stop
blaming yourself and get a hug from loved ones.

☽ ♐
Moon in Sagittarius

JAN

15

THU

♀ ♑ ✳ ♄ ♓
Venus in Capricorn sextile Saturn in Pisces

You want and deserve a lifestyle that combines
your productivity, work and career with
moments of connection with your higher
self and your spirituality. Nobody is healthy
unless these two areas are in balance.

♀ ♑ △ ♅ ℞ ♉
Venus in Capricorn trine Uranus Retrograde in Taurus

Uranus' help can come as an electric shock. Suddenly
you discover an app that can help you to stop wasting
your most precious resource: your quality time with
family and friends. Use technology to optimize your life!

☽ ♐
Moon in Sagittarius

JAN
16
FRI

☽ ♑
Moon in Capricorn

JAN
17
SAT

♀ ♑ ✳ ♆ ♓
Venus in Capricorn sextile Neptune in Pisces

This is a marvellous Saturday for you to slow down a bit and perhaps listen
to some good music or something that connects you with your higher self.

☉ ♑ ✳ ♄ ♓
Sun in Capricorn sextile Saturn in Pisces

I know you'd like to follow your life plan to the letter, but today you
should focus on all those things you always put off for later.

♀ ♒
Venus enters Aquarius until 10 February

You've been feeling sorry for yourself about unfinished work, but take
some time to concentrate on the future – it's just around the corner!

☉ ♑ △ ♅ ℞ ♉
Sun in Capricorn trine Uranus Retrograde in Taurus

Before the day ends, Uranus has one more surprise in store for you. What
is it that you'd like to manifest? Suddenly, it might just fall into your lap!

☽ ♑
Moon in Capricorn

T F S S M T W T F S S M T W T F S S M T W T F S S M T W T F S
1 2 3 4 5 6 7 8 9 10 11 12 13 14 15 16 17 18 19 20 21 22 23 24 25 26 27 28 29 30 31

צב

ה·י·ו·ה

Meditation for the month of Sh'vat
Scan with your eyes from right to left

C A P R I C O R N

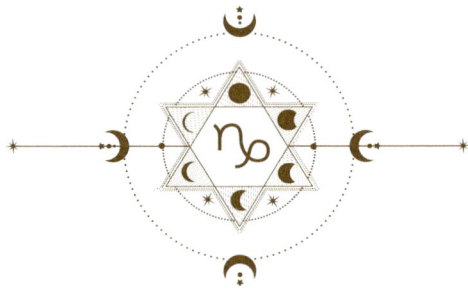

18 JANUARY – 7:52PM (UTC) – NEW MOON 28° CAPRICORN

Los Angeles (UTC –8) • New York (UTC –5) • London (UTC +0)

Paris (UTC +1) • Sydney (UTC +11)

IN THE NEXT SIX MONTHS I WILL MANIFEST ...

Security	Long-term goals	Merit
Ambition	Recognition	High states of being
Social status	Planning	Hard work
Career	Financial stability	Reward

JAN

18

SUN

☿ ♂ ♂ ♑
Mercury meets Mars in Capricorn

After such a lively Saturday, it's a Sunday of many meetings. It's a great day to catch up with someone you really want to have an important conversation with. Just watch out for arguments.

● ♑
New Moon 28º in Capricorn at 7:52pm (UTC)

Set your intentions for this New Moon to bring you more simplicity as you fulfil your obligations. The world and the way we work have changed. Aim for a lighter approach when manifesting your goals.

☽ ♒
Moon in Aquarius

☿ ♑ ⚹ ♄ ♓
Mercury in Capricorn sextile Saturn in Pisces

JAN

19

MON

Mercury shows that sometimes the way forward is to hand our worries over to the Universe and wait for better direction.

☿ ♑ △ ♅ ℞ ♉
Mercury in Capricorn trine Uranus Retrograde in Taurus

Once again, Uranus brings up something surprising from your past that you may have forgotten to help you strengthen your faith in the intangible.

☉ ♑ ⚹ ♆ ♓
Sun in Capricorn sextile Neptune in Pisces

Don't schedule any important conversations for today because your concentration on material things will fade as the day progresses. Instead, reflect and be open to messages from the higher dimensions.

☽ ♒
Moon in Aquarius

JAN
20
TUE

☉ ♒
Sun enters Aquarius at 1:45am (UTC)
After focusing so much on your status for 2026, it's time to innovate and look forward!
Today is the perfect time to update your technology and enhance your digital presence.

♀ ☌ ♇ ♒
Venus meets Pluto in Aquarius
The day is full of aspects. Are you ready to access your digital treasure?

♄ ♓ ✳ ♅ ℞ ♉
Saturn in Pisces sextile Uranus Retrograde in Taurus
It's an excellent day for digital ventures focused on healing and faith.

♂ ♑ △ ♅ ℞ ♉
Mars in Capricorn trine Uranus Retrograde in Taurus
Uranus will bring you the technological tools you need to make life easier.

♂ ♑ ✳ ♄ ♓
Mars in Capricorn sextile Saturn in Pisces
Recognize that there is more to life than obtaining material goods.

☿ ♑ ✳ ♆ ♓
Mercury in Capricorn sextile Neptune in Pisces
Open yourself up to receive more messages from your spirit guides.

☿ ♒
Mercury enters Aquarius until 6 February
Focus on the future and your thoughts will gain speed and clarity.

☽ ♒
Moon in Aquarius

JAN
21
WED

☉ ☌ ☿ ♒
Sun meets Mercury in Aquarius

Right at the start of this new chapter, the Sun and
Mercury talk together to align mind and body. All
mental work becomes more expressive and original.

☽ ♓
Moon in Pisces

T	F	S	S	M	T	W	T	F	S	S	M	T	W	T	F	S	S	M	T	W	T	F	S	S	M	T	W	T	F	S
1	2	3	4	5	6	7	8	9	10	11	12	13	14	15	16	17	18	19	20	21	22	23	24	25	26	27	28	29	30	31

AQUARIUS

AIR

URANUS

20 JANUARY
1:45AM (UTC)

AQUARIUS

MODE Fixed	**ELEMENT** Air	**RULING PLANET** Uranus	

CRYSTAL Cornelian   **BACH FLOWER REMEDY** Water Violet

PRINCIPLE Positive   **OPPOSITE SIGN** Leo

AQUARIUS AND SIGNS IN LOVE

Aries	♥ ♥ ♥ ♡ ♡	Libra	♥ ♥ ♥ ♥ ♥
Taurus	♥ ♡ ♡ ♡ ♡	Scorpio	♥ ♥ ♡ ♡ ♡
Gemini	♥ ♥ ♥ ♥ ♥	Sagittarius	♥ ♥ ♥ ♥ ♡
Cancer	♥ ♥ ♡ ♡ ♡	Capricorn	♥ ♥ ♡ ♡ ♡
Leo	♥ ♥ ♥ ♥ ♥	Aquarius	♥ ♥ ♥ ♡ ♡
Virgo	♥ ♥ ♡ ♡ ♡	Pisces	♥ ♥ ♡ ♡ ♡

MANTRA I know   **POWER** Vision

KEYWORD Imagination   **ANATOMY** Ankles

LIGHT		**SHADOW**	
Independent	Artistic	Unpredictable	Too fixed opinions
Inventive	Logical	Temperamental	Shy
Individualistic	Eccentric	Bored with details	Radical
Progressive	Intellectual	Cold	Impersonal
	Altruistic		Rebel

JAN

22

THU

☿ ♂ ♇ ♒
Mercury meets Pluto in Aquarius

After aligning with the Sun, Mercury challenges
Pluto to grant you some mental treasures to help
you express yourself to your full potential. It's
an excellent day for talking to your bosses.

☽ ♓
Moon in Pisces

♂ ♑ ✳ ♆ ♓
Mars in Capricorn sextile Neptune in Pisces

JAN

23

FRI

Once again, the cosmos urges you to align your material
ambitions with your beliefs and spiritual foundation.
There is no more room for financial growth without
philanthropy. Donate your time to those in need.

♂ ♒
Mars enters Aquarius until 2 March

Following in the footsteps of the Sun and Mercury, Mars
now wants to put into action a totally innovative plan that
will bring benefits in the near future. It's ready to go!

☉ ♂ ♇ ♒
Sun meets Pluto in Aquarius

On the same day, your essence meets your hidden
power and you need to face your shadows to
avoid being engulfed by them. Time to access your
underworld and discover even more pearls!

☽ ♈
Moon in Aries

T	F	S	S	M	T	W	T	F	S	S	M	T	W	T	F	S	S	M	T	W	T	F	S	S	M	T	W	T	F	S
1	2	3	4	5	6	7	8	9	10	11	12	13	14	15	16	17	18	19	20	21	22	23	24	25	26	27	28	29	30	31

JAN
24
SAT

☽ ♈
Moon in Aries

JAN
25
SUN

☽ ♉
Moon in Taurus

T F S S M T W T F S S M T W T F S S M T W T F S S M T W T F S
1 2 3 4 5 6 7 8 9 10 11 12 13 14 15 16 17 18 19 20 21 22 23 24 25 26 27 28 29 30 31

JAN
26
MON

Ψ ♈
Neptune enters Aries until 2039

A historic moment in heaven is when one of the great planets changes position and takes on a new leadership role. Neptune moving into Aries promises a personal revolution in your beliefs and your individuality. Momentous advances in chemistry and discoveries in medicine may help us address and heal the mental illnesses we've been experiencing since 2020.

◐ ♉
First Quarter 6º in Taurus at 04:48am (UTC)

This Waning Moon in Taurus may be the balm you need to stop relying on the material world and find relief and security in meaningful, intangible things. Your greatest asset is your big heart.

JAN
27
TUE

♂ ♂ ♇ ♒
Mars meets Pluto in Aquarius

It's an intense Tuesday filled with great revelations. This planetary encounter could be the Universe showing you that your actions matter. You may not know how to act in certain new situations, but simply trust in your inner power and your personal compass to see you through.

☽ ♊
Moon in Gemini

JAN
28
WED

☽ ♊
Moon in Gemini

JAN
29
THU

☿ ☌ ♀ ♒
Mercury meets Venus in Aquarius

These two best friends get together to discuss a fair
and balanced future. An excellent way to discuss
sustainable policies in both your work and personal life.
There's no more time to spend on any kind of toxicity,
so move forward for the sake of your mental health.

☽ ♋
Moon in Cancer

T	F	S	S	M	T	W	T	F	S	S	M	T	W	T	F	S	S	M	T	W	T	F	S	S	M	T	W	T	F	S
1	2	3	4	5	6	7	8	9	10	11	12	13	14	15	16	17	18	19	20	21	22	23	24	25	26	27	28	29	30	31

JAN
30
FRI

☾ ♋
Moon in Cancer

JAN
31
SAT

☾ ♋
Moon in Cancer

MON	TUE	WED
02	03	04
09	10	11
◗ ♏		
16	17 ANNULAR ECLIPSE	18
	● ♒	☉ ♓
23	24	25
	◗ ♊	

FEBRUARY

The following are the planetary changes that will happen this month

VENUS

MOVES TO ♓ 10 FEB

SATURN

MOVES TO ♈ 14 FEB

SUN

MOVES TO ♓ 18 FEB

THU	FRI	SAT	SUN
			01 ○ ♌
05	06	07	08
12	13	14	15
19	20	21	22
26	27	28	

FEB

01

SUN

○ ♌
Full Moon 13º in Leo at 10:09pm (UTC)

February is already off to a festive start with this Full
Moon guiding you to access your inner child. Celebrate
your talents in a big way – the busiest month of the
year has just ended and you have a blank sheet of
paper to write your history on. Which talent would
you like to practise more in the coming days?

☆

FEB

02

MON

☽ ♌
Moon in Leo

S M T W T F S S M T W T F S S M T W T F S S M T W T F S
1 2 3 4 5 6 7 8 9 10 11 12 13 14 15 16 17 18 19 20 21 22 23 24 25 26 27 28

FEB
03
TUE

☽ ♍
Moon in Virgo

FEB
04
WED

♅ St D ♉
Uranus Stations Direct in 27º Taurus

Finally, after long months in retrograde, Uranus awakens
in the Aquarian season, prompting us to put our digital
plan for 2026 into practice. What technologies have you
left idle, waiting for the green light from the Universe?

☽ ♍
Moon in Virgo

FEB
05
THU

♅ ☽ ♉
Uranus Direct in Taurus

For five months you've been waiting to accelerate your technological paths, and from today onward everything will finally be easier. See which technologies you'd like to invest your attention in and review your digital strategies for 2026. Today, we begin the farewell party for Uranus in Taurus.

☽ ♎
Moon in Libra

FEB
06
FRI

☿ ♒ □ ♅ ♉
Mercury in Aquarius squares Uranus in Taurus

Uranus' first conversation is with Mercury who is there, in one of his houses, thinking about a sustainable future. Make a to-do list for everything that involves your roles in society – physical and digital. It's time to take better care of yourself and the planet you call home.

☽ ♎
Moon in Libra

FEB
07
SAT

☽ ♏
Moon in Scorpio

FEB
08
SUN

♀ ♒ □ ♅ ♉
Venus in Aquarius squares Uranus in Taurus

Venus and Uranus exchange houses and talk about how to
further their values in society. It's time to pursue collective
achievements rather than just personal ones. Try to find
your self-worth while surfing the collective unconscious.

☽ ♏
Moon in Scorpio

FEB

09

MON

◗ ♏

Last Quarter 20º in Scorpio at 12:43pm (UTC)

Speaking of the collective, today's a good day
to abandon selfish habits and embrace the
vulnerability that comes with focusing on yourself.
Take this opportunity to exfoliate your old skin
and reappear fresh and rejuvenated in public.

FEB

10

TUE

♀ ♓

Venus enters Pisces until 6 March

It's Venus' turn to exalt herself in beauty and
sensitivity. This is the time for artistic practices such
as singing, dancing, music, painting and fine art.
It's time to feel like the goddess of your own story.

☽ ♐

Moon in Sagittarius

☽ ♐
Moon in Sagittarius

☿ ☌ ☊ ♓
Mercury meets North Node in Pisces

Signs from the Universe tell you whether or not you're on the right track. If everything doesn't seem to be working in your favour, perhaps it's a message from the angels to change course and set your sights on something higher. Have trust!

☽ ♑
Moon in Capricorn

FEB
13
FRI

☽ ♑
Moon in Capricorn

FEB
14
SAT

♄ ♈
Saturn enters Aries until 2028

It's a powerful Saturday! In fewer than 20 days,
one of the greats enters Aries again, the sign of
fire, action and impulsiveness. This is a transit
that can shake up society, bringing everything
that makes our blood boil to the surface. Now is a
good time to break free from stagnation and take
charge of your responsibilities. No more being a
victim – you're now the hero of your own narrative.

☽ ♑
Moon in Capricorn

FEB

15

SUN

☽ ♒
Moon in Aquarius

FEB

16

MON

☉ ♒ □ ♅ ♉
Sun in Aquarius squares Uranus in Taurus

This brings a sudden shift in perspective, altering
everything we once considered a fixed value. Once again,
the collective is demanding our attention, this time through
the way we take care of the planet and our role as a living
organism in this cosmos. Something completely unexpected
might occur today. Let the Universe surprise you!

☿ ♓ △ ♃ ℞ ♋
Mercury in Pisces trine Jupiter Retrograde in Cancer

Today is the day to believe in a greater force, to trust
that a higher consciousness can and should guide
us as a community. A blessing is about to happen
in your life, despite all the chaos. Open your eyes
and your heart to receive this nourishment.

☽ ♒
Moon in Aquarius

S M T W T F S S M T W T F S S M T W T F S S M T W T F S
1 2 3 4 5 6 7 8 9 10 11 12 13 14 15 16 17 18 19 20 21 22 23 24 25 26 27 28

FEB
17
TUE

New Moon Annular Eclipse 28º in Aquarius at 12:01pm (UTC)

A New Moon eclipse in Aquarius indicates it's time for society to unite and better organize our groups. By working together, we can achieve more than we realize. This collective effort is part of a larger plan, so let's stay united and move forward as one toward a new society.

☽ ♓
Moon in Pisces

FEB
18
WED

☉ ♓
Sun enters Pisces at 3:52pm (UTC)

After the eclipse, the Sun enters Pisces and we ask for mercy and spiritual understanding of all that is happening. Together in prayer we can create miracles in our lives. Don't give up on your faith. Instead, lean on it, talk to your angels and guides, do your meditation and anchor your divine energy here on Earth.

♀ ☌ ☊ ♓
Venus meets North Node in Pisces

There is no more room for selfish and mundane practices. We have to raise our thoughts to the higher dimensions, always asking for the guidance of light. Today, a divine portal opens for us to ask for forgiveness and compassion.

☽ ♓
Moon in Pisces

ק"ג

ה · ה · י · ן

Meditation for the month of Adar
Scan with your eyes from right to left

A Q U A R I U S

17 FEBRUARY – 12:01PM (UTC) – NEW MOON 28° AQUARIUS

Los Angeles (UTC –8) • New York (UTC –5) • London (UTC +0)
Paris (UTC +1) • Sydney (UTC +11)

IN THE NEXT SIX MONTHS I WILL MANIFEST ...

New friendships
Collectivity
New projects
Innovation

The future
Internet and social
Networks
Eccentricity

Detachment
Leaving addictions
Originality
Activism

PISCES

WATER

NEPTUNE

18 FEBRUARY
3:52PM (UTC)

PISCES

MODE Mutable   **ELEMENT** Water   **RULING PLANET** Neptune

CRYSTAL Amethyst   **BACH FLOWER REMEDY** Rock Rose

PRINCIPLE Negative   **OPPOSITE SIGN** Virgo

PISCES AND SIGNS IN LOVE

Aries	♥ ♥ ♥ ♡ ♡	Libra	♥ ♥ ♡ ♡ ♡
Taurus	♥ ♥ ♥ ♥ ♡	Scorpio	♥ ♥ ♥ ♥ ♥
Gemini	♥ ♡ ♡ ♡ ♡	Sagittarius	♥ ♥ ♥ ♥ ♡
Cancer	♥ ♥ ♥ ♡ ♡	Capricorn	♥ ♥ ♥ ♡ ♡
Leo	♥ ♥ ♥ ♥ ♡	Aquarius	♥ ♥ ♡ ♡ ♡
Virgo	♥ ♥ ♥ ♥ ♥	Pisces	♥ ♥ ♥ ♥ ♥

MANTRA I believe   **POWER** Comprehension

KEYWORD Intuition   **ANATOMY** Feet

LIGHT

Compassionate   Intuitive
Charitable   Introspective
Friendly   Musical
Emotional   Artistic
Makes sacrifices Psychic

SHADOW

Procrastinator   Shy
Very talkative   Not practical
Melancholic   Indolent
Pessimistic   Often feels
Emotionally inhibited misunderstood

FEB
19
THU

☽ ♈
Moon in Aries

FEB
20
FRI

♄ ☌ ♆ ♈
Saturn meets Neptune in Aries

Long awaited for the last 36 years, the great summit
of the cosmos is the protagonist of the aspects on
this unpretentious Friday. It's a time to let go of old
illusions and focus on rebuilding our society. Embrace
your spiritual path and connect with nature to ground
the intense energy of the moment. Try walking
barefoot on grass or dipping your feet in salt water
to help manage any confusion or nervousness. Let
go of the old and prepare for spiritual growth.

☽ ♈
Moon in Aries

S M T W T F S S M T W T F S S M T W T F S S M T W T F S
1 2 3 4 5 6 7 8 9 10 11 12 13 14 15 16 17 18 19 20 21 22 23 24 25 26 27 28

FEB

21

SAT

☽ ♉
Moon in Taurus

FEB

22

SUN

♀ ♓ △ ♃ ℞ ♋
Venus in Pisces trine Jupiter Retrograde in Cancer

This is a Sunday to go down in history and ask for
peace! The cause of all human suffering lies in
attachment and desire for material things, so take
advantage of this holy day to connect with what
your soul most desires. Be at peace with yourself
and you will bring peace to all of humanity.

☽ ♉
Moon in Taurus

S M T W T F S S M T W T F S S M T W T F S S M T W T F S
1 2 3 4 5 6 7 8 9 10 11 12 13 14 15 16 17 18 19 20 21 22 23 24 25 26 27 28

FEB
23
MON

☽ ♉
Moon in Taurus

FEB
24
TUE

◗ ♊
First Quarter 5º in Gemini at 12:28pm (UTC)

Consider your social network, strengthen ties
with friends and siblings and try to learn from the
innocence of the youth. Look after the children and
the younger generations who will be the future
of the planet. Do something important today!

FEB
25
WED

☽ ♊
Moon in Gemini

FEB
26
THU

☿ St ℞ ♓
Mercury Stations Retrograde in 22º Pisces

This is Mercury's first retrograde of the year, bringing us
back to our higher consciousness, connecting us with our
faith and the things we do without an agenda. It's an excellent
time to donate your time and effort to the less fortunate.

☽ ♋
Moon in Cancer

♂ ♒ □ ♅ ♉
Mars in Aquarius squares Uranus in Taurus

FEB
27
FRI

With Mercury in Uranus, information is pouring in
from all sides and we need to decide what needs
discussing for the greater good of humanity.

☿ ℞ ♓
Mercury Retrograde in Pisces until 20 March

Stay tuned for all the issues and emotions that will
return to your thoughts over the next few days.

☉ ♂ ☊ ♓
Sun meets North Node in Pisces

The Sun at the eclipse activation point announces a new
stage in our lives emerging in the face of so many events.
The eclipses in Pisces ask us to put aside the role of victim
and take our own responsibility for our spiritual mission on
Earth. What can you do to raise the collective vibration?

☽ ♋
Moon in Cancer

FEB
28
SAT

☿ ℞ ♂ ♀ ♓
Mercury Retrograde meets Venus in Pisces

The best friends' plan needs to be redone and
rethought. It's time to look at everything you have
in your life and give thanks for the opportunity to be
here experiencing all these transformations. If you
can, set aside time for those who need help. Any
good deed, kindness or donation of time is welcome.

☽ ♌
Moon in Leo

S M T W T F S S M T W T F S S M T W T F S S M T W T F S
1 2 3 4 5 6 7 8 9 10 11 12 13 14 15 16 17 18 19 20 21 22 23 24 25 26 27 28

30	31	
02	03 TOTAL ECLIPSE	04
	○ ♍	
09	10	11
		◗ ♐
16	17	18
23	24	25
		◖ ♋

MAR CH

The following
are the planetary
changes that will
happen this month

MARS

MOVES TO ♓ 2 MAR

VENUS

MOVES TO ♈ 6 MAR
MOVES TO ♉ 30 MAR

SUN

MOVES TO ♈ 20 MAR

THU	FRI	SAT	SUN
			01
05	06	07	08
12	13	14	15
19	20 EQUINOX ☉ ♈	21	22
● ♓			
26	27	28	29

MAR

01

SUN

☽ ♌
Moon in Leo

MAR

02

MON

♂ ♓
Mars enters Pisces until 9 April

The plan first proposed by Mercury in Pisces, then revised
by Venus in Pisces, now falls into the hands of Mars, who
will act to make this new spiritual ideal a reality. Get back
to your meditative practices and prayers, anchor your
energy in the divine and share as much as you can.

☽ ♍
Moon in Virgo

MAR
03
TUE

○ ♍
Full Moon Total Eclipse 12º in Virgo at 11:38am (UTC)

What you intended on 21 September last year is
now ready to be shared. It's the right time to serve
a greater purpose, finding a connection with the
divine and the invisible world of prayer. We are all
working to cleanse ourselves of everything that
no longer makes sense in this new society.

MAR
04
WED

♀ ♓ ✳ ♅ ♉
Venus in Pisces sextile Uranus in Taurus

A big surprise could knock on your door today. After all
the hustle and bustle in the sky, something you've been
working on for a while is ready to be enjoyed. Venus
is delighted with your dedication to others over the
last few days, so take credit for your valued efforts.

☽ ♎
Moon in Libra

MAR
05
THU

☉ ♓ △ ♃ ℞ ♋
Sun in Pisces trine Jupiter Retrograde in Cancer

Now it's time for the Sun to acknowledge all its work over the last year. This is a great day to celebrate your joint efforts and all the inner work you've done to reveal a new identity to the world and the people you love the most. It's also a good day to share your faith.

☽ ♎
Moon in Libra

MAR
06
FRI

♀ ♈
Venus enters Aries until 30 March

After so much personal sacrifice, now it's time to think about yourself. Venus in Aries is bold, daring and jumps at what she wants. It could be a good time to shake things up a bit in your love life, whether you're single or in a couple. It's a good time to take a few risks, but beware of overdoing it, especially financially.

☽ ♎
Moon in Libra

S	M	T	W	T	F	S	S	M	T	W	T	F	S	S	M	T	W	T	F	S	S	M	T	W	T	F	S	S	M	T
1	2	3	4	5	6	7	8	9	10	11	12	13	14	15	16	17	18	19	20	21	22	23	24	25	26	27	28	29	30	31

☉ ♂ ☿ ℞ ♓

MAR

07

SAT

Sun meets Mercury Retrograde in Pisces

With so much focus on caring for the planet, it's time to review how we care for ourselves. Today is a good day to please yourself and your senses. If your mental health needs attention, seek out a friend who is a good listener or consult a therapist to share what is troubling you. Connect with your emotions.

♀ ♂ ♆ ♈

Venus meets Neptune in Aries

Venus' first conversation in Aries is with the King of the Seas, who is now stirring up a tsunami of emotions in our lives. It's time to align your courage and ingenuity with your deepest emotions – the ones that have been tormenting you lately. It's not a good day for practical tasks, but rather for working on your sensitive and more artistic side.

☽ ♏

Moon in Scorpio

MAR

08

SUN

♀ ♂ ♄ ♈

Venus meets Saturn in Aries

From now on, everyone entering Aries will have to immerse themselves in Neptune's inspirations, and then salute Saturn and align their self-responsibility and commitments. Check in with yourself to see if all this giving to the community has affected your own stability. Reaffirm to yourself that serving society doesn't mean neglecting your personal needs.

☽ ♏

Moon in Scorpio

MAR
09
MON

☿ ℞ ♓ △ ♃ ℞ ♋
Mercury Retrograde in Pisces trine
Jupiter Retrograde in Cancer

A conversation from the past or a forgotten love
from years ago may come up again on this nostalgic
and needy Monday. Revel in your nostalgia, then
gradually turn your attention and heart to what
you need today. Be present in your life now!

☽ ♐
Moon in Sagittarius

MAR
10
TUE

♀ ♈ ✳ ♇ ♒
Venus in Aries sextile Pluto in Aquarius

It takes courage to share your talents and perform to your
greatest potential. Venus in Aries indicates ambitions and she
wants you to reach higher levels in life. It's a good time for
daring proposals that highlight your self-worth even more.

☽ ♐
Moon in Sagittarius

S M T W T F S S M T W T F S S M T W T F S S M T W T F S S M T
1 2 3 4 5 6 7 8 9 10 11 12 13 14 15 16 17 18 19 20 21 22 23 24 25 26 27 28 29 30 31

MAR
11
WED

♃ St D ♋
Jupiter Stations Direct in 15º Cancer

Everything that has been stuck since November 2025 now seems to flow intensely. The first few days can be intense and the tears may flow without warning. Let these emotions come to the surface. Perhaps they are what the planet needs to ignite its energy, connect with our heart chakra and help us evolve as a cosmic family.

Last Quarter 20º in Sagittarius at 9:38am (UTC)

Put aside the need to lecture, showcase your philosophy or be a teacher. Instead, embrace the humble role of an apprentice. This is a time to reconnect and feel, so keep an open mind and a warm heart.

MAR
12
THU

♃ St D ♋
Jupiter Stations Direct in Cancer

You will feel relieved as you learn to improve your emotional intelligence, because there are no more obstacles stopping you from progressing. Go for it!

☽ ♑
Moon in Capricorn

MAR

13
FRI

♂ ☌ ☊ ♓
Mars meets North Node in Pisces

It's a wonderful Friday to start acting with more purpose
and directing your energy toward a higher mission.
Connect now with your spiritual obligations – we are
here to work on and raise Earth vibrations, not just to
suffer and ask for mercy. Practise your faith daily.

☽ ♑
Moon in Capricorn

MAR

14
SAT

☽ ♒
Moon in Aquarius

MAR

15

SUN

☿ R ♂ ♂ ♓
Mercury Retrograde meets Mars in Pisces

After rethinking, retracing your steps, rewriting your story and reworking your neural connections, it's now time to plan your next steps based on what your spirit feels. Prepare to start again once Mercury awakens.

☽ ♒
Moon in Aquarius

MAR

16

MON

☽ ♓
Moon in Pisces

MAR
17
TUE

☽ ♓
Moon in Pisces

MAR
18
WED

♀ ♈ □ ♃ ♋
Venus in Aries squares Jupiter in Cancer

Your ancestors made room for you to shine today. Family issues
may be holding you back from expressing yourself, but think about
how far you've come since the beginning of the year. Rethink your
rebelliousness and welcome those who still need your help.

☉ ♓ ✳ ♅ ♉
Sun in Pisces sextile Uranus in Taurus

In the final days of the Pisces season, an unexpected event may
comfort your heart. Everything you do without expecting anything in
return surprises you in new ways.
All the energy you give comes back to you even stronger.

☽ ♓
Moon in Pisces

S M T W T F S S M T W T F S S M T W T F S S M T W T F S S M T
1 2 3 4 5 6 **7** **8** 9 10 11 12 13 **14** **15** 16 17 18 19 20 **21** **22** 23 24 25 26 27 **28** **29** 30 31

MAR
19
THU

● ♓
New Moon 28º in Pisces at 1:23am (UTC)

As the Sun bids farewell to the Piscean seas, there's
one last New Moon, which will take on the force
of a great eclipse in August. Once again, it's time
to work with the positive, sensitive, supportive and
artistic side of Pisces. All great work involving music,
photography, cinema, audiovisuals and fine art will
gain immense strength. Don't make war, make art!

☽ ♈
Moon in Aries

MAR
20
FRI

☉ ♈
Sun enters Aries at 2:46pm (UTC)

Happy Astrological New Year! The arrival of a new season is the perfect
time to reset our emotions and channel our energy toward our yearly
goals. If you feel nervous, take part in high-impact sports to relieve anxiety.
Dry your tears, step out of hiding and start tackling new challenges.

☿ St D ♓
Mercury Stations Direct in 8º Pisces

Now is a good time to reflect on the negative emotions of
the last month. Today, you also have the green light to sign
contracts, as long as they are fully in tune with your heart.

Equinoxes
Spring Equinox – Northern Hemisphere
Autumn Equinox – Southern Hemisphere
Ostara Festival – Bring flowers to your altar
and paint eggs to celebrate

☽ ♈
Moon in Aries

S	M	T	W	T	F	S	S	M	T	W	T	F	S	S	M	T	W	T	F	S	S	M	T	W	T	F	S	S	M	T
1	2	3	4	5	6	7	8	9	10	11	12	13	14	15	16	17	18	19	20	21	22	23	24	25	26	27	28	29	30	31

MAR
21
SAT

☿ D ♓
Mercury Direct in Pisces

Take advantage of this Saturday to organize your emotions
and prepare to make decisions that have been unclear
for the last 20 days. Go ahead and make commitments
to your spirituality and meditation practices.

☽ ♉
Moon in Taurus

MAR
22
SUN

♂ ♓ △ ♃ ♋
Mars in Pisces trine Jupiter in Cancer

It's an inspiring Sunday because we are searching for
more meaningful intentions than we once pursued.
It's time to seek emotional security, working internally
on emotional wounds so that we can understand
ourselves better and direct our fragile nature toward
more solid perceptions of who we really are.

☉ ♂ ♆ ♈
Sun meets Neptune in Aries

Pure energy from the divine flame provides authentic
inspiration for your creativity. Visualize your ideal
future and collect the images you'd like to experience
in your reality over the next six months. Dream big!

☽ ♉
Moon in Taurus

S M T W T F S S M T W T F S S M T W T F S S M T W T F S S M T
1 2 3 4 5 6 7 8 9 10 11 12 13 14 15 16 17 18 19 20 21 22 23 24 25 26 27 28 29 30 31

Meditation for the month of Nissan
Scan with your eyes from right to left

P I S C E S

19 MARCH – 1:23AM (UTC) NEW MOON 28° PISCES

Los Angeles (UTC –8) • New York (UTC –5) • London (UTC +0)

Paris (UTC +1) • Sydney (UTC +11)

IN THE NEXT SIX MONTHS I WILL MANIFEST...

Inspiration	Transcendence	Intuition
Unconditional love	Compassion	Altruism
Enlightenment	Spirituality	Philanthropy
Mysticism	Collective unconscious	Charity

♈

ARIES

△
FIRE

♂
MARS

20 MARCH
2:46PM (UTC)

ARIES

MODE Cardinal   **ELEMENT** Fire   **RULING PLANET** Mars

CRYSTAL Pyrite   **BACH FLOWER REMEDY** Impatiens

PRINCIPLE Positive   **OPPOSITE SIGN** Libra

ARIES AND SIGNS IN LOVE

Aries	♥ ♥ ♥ ♡ ♡	Libra	♥ ♥ ♥ ♥ ♥
Taurus	♥ ♡ ♡ ♡ ♡	Scorpio	♥ ♥ ♡ ♡ ♡
Gemini	♥ ♥ ♥ ♥ ♥	Sagittarius	♥ ♥ ♥ ♥ ♡
Cancer	♥ ♥ ♡ ♡ ♡	Capricorn	♥ ♥ ♡ ♡ ♡
Leo	♥ ♥ ♥ ♥ ♡	Aquarius	♥ ♥ ♥ ♡ ♡
Virgo	♥ ♥ ♡ ♡ ♡	Pisces	♥ ♥ ♡ ♡ ♡

MANTRA I am   **POWER** Action

KEYWORD Assert   **ANATOMY** Head, Face, Brain

LIGHT
Pioneer   Independent
Competitive   Dynamic
Impulsive   Living in the present
Courageous   Fast

SHADOW
Dominating   Arrogant
Irascible   "Me first"
Violent   Rude
Intolerant   Has no persistence

MAR
23
MON

☽ ♊
Moon in Gemini

MAR
24
TUE

☽ ♊
Moon in Gemini

S M T W T F S S M T W T F S S M T W T F S S M T W T F S S M T
1 2 3 4 5 6 7 8 9 10 11 12 13 14 15 16 17 18 19 20 21 22 23 24 25 26 27 28 29 30 31

MAR
25
WED

⊙ ☌ ♄ ♈
Sun meets Saturn in Aries

It's time to set achievable goals between where you
are today and where you want to be. Saturn helps
you establish the stages of manifesting a dream.
Choose a goal and work backward, listing the stages
of completion until you achieve it. Happy planning!

⊙ ♈ ✳ ♇ ♒
Sun in Aries sextile Pluto in Aquarius

Take this opportunity to also reflect on who your
big dream involves. Who are the people you
need to manifest what you've always wanted?
Make important contacts, even if it's just to
strengthen ties until the vital breakthrough.

◗ ♋
First Quarter 5º in Cancer at 7:18pm (UTC)

All of this year's transits ask you to check if
everything is aligned with what your heart desires.
Seeking emotional security is a daily task, as is
verifying that you are confident enough to take
each step toward realizing your intentions.

MAR
26
THU

☽ ♋
Moon in Cancer

MAR
27
FRI

☽ ♌
Moon in Leo

MAR
28
SAT

♄ ♈ ✳ ♇ ♒
Saturn in Aries sextile Pluto in Aquarius

The big manifestation plan for 2026 doesn't give you
a break at weekends. Ensure that your goals align
with your heart and what you're willing to do, risk and
face to achieve them. A good individual plan can grow
into something that benefits an entire community.
Expand your manifestations to include more people.

☽ ♌
Moon in Leo

MAR
29
SUN

☽ ♍
Moon in Virgo

MAR
30
MON

♀ ♉
Venus enters Taurus until 24 April

Before we finish the busiest month so far, Venus returns to one
of her homes, takes off her heels and grounds her energy in
nature. Focus carefully on where you are directing your attention,
both materially and spiritually, and take stock of your finances,
as this is the best time to invest resources successfully.

☽ ♍
Moon in Virgo

S M T W T F S S M T W T F S S M T W T F S S M T W T F S S M T
1 2 3 4 5 6 7 8 9 10 11 12 13 14 15 16 17 18 19 20 21 22 23 24 25 26 27 28 29 30 31

MAR
31
TUE

☽ ♍
Moon in Virgo

MON	TUE	WED
		01
06	07	08
13	14	15
20	21	22
☉ ♉		
27	28	29

The following are the planetary changes that will happen this month

MARS

MOVES TO ♈ 9 APR

MERCURY

MOVES TO ♈ 15 APR

SUN

MOVES TO ♉ 20 APR

VENUS

MOVES TO ♊ 24 APR

URANUS

MOVES TO ♊ 25 APR

THU	FRI	SAT	SUN
02 ○ ♎	03	04	05
09	10 ◑ ♑	11	12
16	17 ● ♈	18	19
23	24 ◑ ♌	25	26
30			

APR
01
WED

☽ ♎
Moon in Libra

APR
02
THU

○ ♎
Full Moon 12º in Libra 2:12am (UTC)

The weekend is approaching and this Full Moon makes
us want to socialize, feast our eyes on beautiful things,
delight in fine art, seduce and be seduced. Which
relationship in your life do you see as being out of kilter
today? Take the opportunity to rebalance your moods.

W T F S S M T W T F S S M T W T F S S M T W T F S S M T W T
1 2 3 4 5 6 7 8 9 10 11 12 13 14 15 16 17 18 19 20 21 22 23 24 25 26 27 28 29 30

APR

03

FRI

☿ ♓ △ ♃ ♋
Mercury in Pisces trine Jupiter in Cancer

The planets have already changed their energy, but Mercury is still focused on how to help others and improve the world through art and creativity. Invest in tasks that involve caring for others and their mental health.

♀ ♉ □ ♇ ♒
Venus in Taurus squares Pluto in Aquarius

The test here is to distinguish between desires driven by the ego and those driven by the soul. To take responsibility for your community, you need to feel safe. Reflect on what you want and what will have the greatest impact on the people you live with.

☽ ♏
Moon in Scorpio

APR

04

SAT

☽ ♏
Moon in Scorpio

APR
05
SUN

☉ ♈ □ ♃ ♋
Sun in Aries squares Jupiter in Cancer

This is another aspect that requires you to balance
your individualism with your emotional security. You
might face conflicts between your goals and meeting
family or emotional needs. Try to find a balance
between your own desires and the needs of others.

♀ ♉ ✳ ☊ ♓
Venus in Taurus sextile North Node in Pisces

After reflecting on her conversation with Pluto,
Venus seems to have decided what she wants,
what she deserves and what would have a
positive impact on her life. It's a day for receiving
divine inspiration. Connect with your angels!

☽ ♐
Moon in Sagittarius

APR
06
MON

☽ ♐
Moon in Sagittarius

W T F S S M T W T F S S M T W T F S S M T W T F S S M T W T
1 2 3 **4** **5** 6 7 8 9 10 **11** **12** 13 14 15 16 17 **18** **19** 20 21 22 23 24 **25** **26** 27 28 29 30

APR
07
TUE

☽ ♐
Moon in Sagittarius

APR
08
WED

♂ ♓ ✳ ♅ ♉
Mars in Pisces sextile Uranus in Taurus

This latest aspect of Mars in Pisces combines
the intuitive with the innovative to help you
create sustainable projects. Is there something
you long to make a reality? Any shelved ideas
that you feel it's time to bring to fruition? From
tomorrow you will gain the strength and courage
to go after your dreams. Think carefully about how
you can help make the world a better place.

☽ ♑
Moon in Capricorn

WT F S S M T W T F S S M T W T F S S M T W T F S S M T W T
1 2 3 **4 5** 6 7 8 9 10 **11 12** 13 14 15 16 17 **18 19** 20 21 22 23 24 **25 26** 27 28 29 30

APR
09
THU

♂ ♈
Mars enters Aries until 18 May

A radical change of energy will shake up your next
40 days. The will to act is so strong that you can
feel a nervousness creeping in. Use this energy
productively by engaging in a hands-on project.
It's an excellent time to get back into high-impact
sports. A run around a park could be just the
remedy you need for a good night's sleep.

☽ ♑
Moon in Capricorn

APR
10
FRI

◑ ♑
Last Quarter 20º in Capricorn at 4:52am (UTC)

This Friday let go of your need to have everything
under control and your false belief that you need
to work hard and enjoy little leisure and rest. Your
body needs to cope with all the physical challenges
and your mental health requires regular breaks.
Take a minute to contemplate nature this weekend.

☽ ♒
Moon in Aquarius

W	T	F	S	S	M	T	W	T	F	S	S	M	T	W	T	F	S	S	M	T	W	T	F	S	S	M	T	W	T
1	2	3	4	5	6	7	8	9	10	11	12	13	14	15	16	17	18	19	20	21	22	23	24	25	26	27	28	29	30

APR
11
SAT

☽ ♒
Moon in Aquarius

APR
12
SUN

☽ ♒
Moon in Aquarius

APR
13
MON

♂ ☌ ♆ ♈
Mars meets Neptune in Aries

It's a great day for creative activities and for turning imaginative ideas into reality. But it can also lead to confusion, unrealistic goals or evasive practices. You need to be beware of illusions and ensure that your actions are based on clear and realistic foundations.

♀ ♉ ✳ ♃ ♋
Venus in Taurus sextile Jupiter in Cancer

To soften the start of this week, this aspect can bring us the support structure we need to experience love, beauty and abundance in the realms of the heart, as well as in material life. It encourages harmonious relationships, creative expression and a deep appreciation for the comforts of home and family life.

☽ ♓
Moon in Pisces

APR
14
TUE

☿ ♓ ✳ ♅ ♉
Mercury in Pisces sextile Uranus in Taurus

This aspect encourages you to find unique and creative solutions to problems related to technology. It often involves a blend of intuition and innovative thinking. Today, you might experience sudden insights and unconventional ideas that are both daring and inspiring. Use this opportunity to tap into your intuition and apply it practically in the digital world.

☽ ♓
Moon in Pisces

W T F S S M T W T F S S M T W T F S S M T W T F S S M T W T
1 2 3 4 5 6 7 8 9 10 11 12 13 14 15 16 17 18 19 20 21 22 23 24 25 26 27 28 29 30

APR
15
WED

☿ ♈
Mercury enters Aries until 3 May

Finally, after long months in Pisces,
Mercury enters Aries and we receive a
boost of courage to express ourselves.
It's an excellent time to know what you
want to say in conversations you've
been avoiding or negotiations you need
to make. All the intellectual pursuits
that have been at a standstill due to
retrogradation now gain rocket power.

☽ ♈
Moon in Aries

APR
16
THU

♂ ♈ ✳ ♇ ♒
Mars in Aries sextile Pluto in Aquarius

It's Mars' turn to receive a powerful push and
encourage you to act boldly in the community.
Your project involving a group of friends could
gain prominence or you could receive help from
someone very important and with unparalleled
impact. It's an excellent time for moving the
pieces on the board. Today is checkmate day!

☽ ♈
Moon in Aries

W T F S S M T W T F S S M T W T F S S M T W T F S S M T W T
1 2 3 4 5 6 7 8 9 10 11 12 13 14 15 16 17 18 19 20 21 22 23 24 25 26 27 28 29 30

APR
17
FRI

☿ ☌ ♆ ♈
Mercury meets Neptune in Aries

Today's powerful aspect combines imaginative intuition with assertive communication. Mercury receives the Neptunian inspiration to bring visionary ideas to life, but you'll need emotional balance to fully benefit from these insights.

● ♈
New Moon 27º in Aries at 11:52am (UTC)

Opening a new chapter in the Zodiac wheel, the 12 days that follow contain the seeds for the next 12 months. Watch your thoughts this season. Avoid being reactive or impulsive and try not to be selfish. In 12 days' time we'll see if we can celebrate or need to continue improving ourselves as human beings.

☽ ♉
Moon in Taurus

APR
18
SAT

☿ ♈ ✳ ♇ ♒
Mercury in Aries sextile Pluto in Aquarius

Today, you can gain deep insights into complex issues and understand underlying dynamics once and for all. It's also an excellent week to talk to your superiors – people who will be able to help you and who are currently in a higher position than you. Good luck!

☽ ♉
Moon in Taurus

פן

י · ה · ה · ו

Meditation for the month of Iyar
Scan with your eyes from right to left

A R I E S

17 APRIL – 11:52AM (UTC) – NEW MOON 27° ARIES

Los Angeles (UTC –7) • New York (UTC –4) • London (UTC +0)
Paris (UTC +1) • Sydney (UTC +10)

IN THE NEXT SIX MONTHS I WILL MANIFEST ...

New cycle	Passion	Acceptance of risks
Energy of beginnings	New image	Self-challenge
Impulse	Initiative and proactivity	New developments
Strength and courage	Leadership	Physical training

APR
19
SUN

♂ ♂ ♄ ♈
Mars meets Saturn in Aries

Today, the emphasis is on action and energy with discipline and structure. If you've lacked motivation, now is the time to act without hesitation. Consider starting a new exercise plan to boost both mental and physical health. Take advantage of this and don't miss the target in front of you. Hit the bullseye!

☽ ♊
Moon in Gemini

☉ ♉
Sun enters Taurus at 1:39am (UTC)

The Sun enters Taurus, stabilizing our energy and encouraging us to develop the foundations we need to overcome challenges. It's a good time for a nature getaway, reviewing finances and exploring alternative therapies to enhance your wellbeing.

APR
20
MON

☿ ♂ ♄ ♈
Mercury meets Saturn in Aries

Today, you might feel physically sluggish but mentally alert. Use this time to take action and reassess your priorities for the month.

☿ ♂ ♂ ♈
Mercury meets Mars in Aries

Visualize every task you need to do today. You need to have a vision and not waste time with thoughtless and impulsive actions. Although your mind is active, ensure your actions follow a logical order. Structure and plan effectively.

☽ ♊
Moon in Gemini

APR

21
TUE

☽ ♋
Moon in Cancer

APR

22
WED

☽ ♋
Moon in Cancer

W T F S S M T W T F S S M T W T F S S M T W T F S S M T W T
1 2 3 **4** 5 6 7 8 9 10 **11 12** 13 14 15 16 17 **18 19** 20 21 22 23 24 **25 26** 27 28 29 30

TAURUS

EARTH

VENUS

20 APRIL
1:39AM (UTC)

TAURUS

MODE Fixed   **ELEMENT** Earth   **RULING PLANET** Venus

CRYSTAL Emerald   **BACH FLOWER REMEDY** Gentian

PRINCIPLE Negative   **OPPOSITE SIGN** Scorpio

TAURUS AND SIGNS IN LOVE

Aries	♥ ♡ ♡ ♡ ♡	Libra	♥ ♥ ♥ ♥ ♡
Taurus	♥ ♥ ♥ ♥ ♡	Scorpio	♥ ♥ ♥ ♥ ♥
Gemini	♥ ♥ ♡ ♡ ♡	Sagittarius	♥ ♡ ♡ ♡ ♡
Cancer	♥ ♥ ♥ ♡ ♡	Capricorn	♥ ♥ ♥ ♡ ♡
Leo	♥ ♥ ♥ ♥ ♡	Aquarius	♥ ♥ ♡ ♡ ♡
Virgo	♥ ♥ ♥ ♥ ♥	Pisces	♥ ♥ ♥ ♥ ♡

MANTRA I have   **POWER** Stability

KEYWORD Possess   **ANATOMY** Neck, Ears, Vocal cords, Thyroid, Tongue, Throat, Mouth, Tonsils

LIGHT
Patient
Conservative
Sensual
Scrupulous
Stable
Trustworthy
Practical
Loyal

SHADOW
Self-indulgent
Stubborn
Slow
Prone to discussion
Irascible
Possessive
Gluttonous
Materialistic

APR
23
THU

☽ ♌
Moon in Leo

♀ ☌ ♅ ♉
Venus meets Uranus in Taurus

APR
24
FRI

This is a good Friday to promote your talents through social networks, make strategic investments in technology and improve your digital image. But beware of extravagant purchases! Going on your cellphone at the wrong time could lead you to gambling your money away.

♀ ♊
Venus enters Gemini until 19 May

Venus wastes no time in rushing off to the party in Gemini. Enjoy socializing and meeting new people but, again, keep an eye on your spending as the party season begins.

◑ ♌
First Quarter 3º in Leo at 2:32am (UTC)

This crescent Moon in Leo increases our desire to bring out our inner child to party and dance. Enjoy yourself, but avoid exaggerating your importance or flaunting more than you have. Show only your best side today!

APR

25

SAT

☉ ♉ □ ♇ ♒
Sun in Taurus squares Pluto in Aquarius

The stable, safety-oriented energy of the Sun in Taurus squared with the intense, transformative energy of Pluto in Aquarius can lead to a challenging but potentially life-changing interaction. An encounter with someone who touches you deeply, or who you thought was impossible to reach, may surprise you.

♅ ♊
Uranus enters Gemini until 2033

Uranus finally leaves the sign of Taurus 50 minutes after midnight. After moving in and out of Gemini last year, Uranus now enters the sign of communications for good and promises to shake things up radically. Embrace change and strengthen your critical thinking to navigate this dynamic period.

☽ ♌

Moon in Leo

APR

26

SUN

☉ ♉ ✳ ☊ ♓
Sun in Taurus sextile North Node in Pisces

On this busy Sunday, you may feel your purpose blossoming right before your eyes. A restless energy of transformation and drastic change is beginning to emerge. And that's just the start of your personal revolution!

♀ ♊ ✳ ♆ ♈
Venus in Gemini sextile Neptune in Aries

Venus wants to flirt with the new, while Neptune insists on daydreaming. Enjoy romantic moments but keep realistic expectations and clear communication.

☿ ♈ □ ♃ ♋
Mercury in Aries squares Jupiter in Cancer

This is another opportunity to share your opinion, taking care not to hurt other people's feelings. Remain patient, take a deep breath and convey your inner truth.

☽ ♍

Moon in Virgo

W	T	F	S	S	M	T	W	T	F	S	S	M	T	W	T	F	S	S	M	T	W	T	F	S	S	M	T	W	T
1	2	3	4	5	6	7	8	9	10	11	12	13	14	15	16	17	18	19	20	21	22	23	24	25	26	27	28	29	30

APR
27
MON

☽ ♍
Moon in Virgo

APR
28
TUE

♀ ♊ △ ♇ ♒
Venus in Gemini trine Pluto in Aquarius

After the weekend's gossip, this aspect helps you connect
assertively in relationships. Focus on developing emotional
intelligence and empathy for better understanding and harmony.
Be clear about what you want from every interaction.

☽ ♎
Moon in Libra

W T F S S M T W T F S S M T W T F S S M T W T F S S M T W T
1 2 3 **4 5** 6 7 8 9 10 **11 12** 13 14 15 16 17 **18 19** 20 21 22 23 24 **25 26** 27 28 29 30

APR

29

WED

♀ ♊ □ ☊ ♓
Venus in Gemini squares North Node in Pisces

Today, you might discover that you want to make
a big impact on society. An ambitious desire that
connects education, the arts and communication
is all your team needs. Make important contacts
– the Universe will be guiding conversations
and thoughts to a new and higher level.

☽ ♎
Moon in Libra

APR

30

THU

☽ ♏
Moon in Scorpio

MON	TUE	WED
04	05	06
11	12	13
18	19	20
25	26	27

MAY

The following
are the planetary
changes that will
happen this month

MERCURY

MOVES TO ♉ 3 MAY

MOVES TO ♊ 17 MAY

MARS

MOVES TO ♉ 18 MAY

VENUS

MOVES TO ♋ 19 MAY

SUN

MOVES TO ♊ 21 MAY

THU	FRI	SAT	SUN
	01	02	03
	○ ♏		
07	08	09	10
		◐ ♒	
14	15	16	17
		● ♉	
21	22	23	24
☉ ♊		◑ ♍	
28	29	30	31
			○ ♐

MAY
01
FRI

○ ♏
Full Moon 11º in Scorpio at 5:23pm (UTC)

The most intense Full Moon of the year, the Wesak
Moon is an excellent time for you to finalize a chapter,
achieve greater understanding through healing and raise
your consciousness toward what really matters. Hidden
emotions tend to surface in full force. Let them flow!

MAY
02
SAT

☽ ♏
Moon in Scorpio

MAY

03

SUN

☿ ♉
Mercury enters Taurus until 17 May

To get the week off to a good start, Mercury sets foot in the most stable sign of the Zodiac, urging you to anchor your thoughts and lay the foundations for your goals. Organize your finances and plan your steps to create even more security along the way.

☽ ♐
Moon in Sagittarius

MAY

04

MON

☽ ♐
Moon in Sagittarius

MAY
05
TUE

♂ ♈ □ ♃ ♋
Mars in Aries squares Jupiter in Cancer

We can only expand our consciousness by
considering our feelings and connections.
Learn to focus on your personal goals
without losing sight of your emotions.

☿ ♉ □ ♇ ♒
Mercury in Taurus squares Pluto in Aquarius

Today is a busy Tuesday before Pluto
goes into retrograde. Mercury seeks clear
thinking, but you need to address your
shadows and consider other viewpoints.

☿ ♉ ⚹ ☊ ♓
Mercury in Taurus sextile North Node in Pisces

It's a day to find security in what you dream
and imagine for the future. And an excellent
time to download the greatest insights from
the cosmos into the physical realm.

☽ ♑
Moon in Capricorn

MAY
06
WED

♇ St ℞ ♒
Pluto Stations Retrograde in 5° Aquarius

Pluto is preparing for his annual rest and is urging
us to revisit all the shadows we carry when we
access the collective unconscious. We have five
months to analyse all the different points of view.

☽ ♑
Moon in Capricorn

MAY
07
THU

♇ ℞ ♒

Pluto Retrograde in Aquarius until 16 October

All Pluto retrogrades open portals to our
subconscious to access the layers that lie beneath
the surface. Today is excellent for going deeper
into any work that involves research, technology or
group work. Take the time to consult an expert.

☽ ♑

Moon in Capricorn

MAY
08
FRI

☽ ♒

Moon in Aquarius

F	S	S	M	T	W	T	F	S	S	M	T	W	T	F	S	S	M	T	W	T	F	S	S	M	T	W	T	F	S	S
1	2	3	4	5	6	7	8	9	10	11	12	13	14	15	16	17	18	19	20	21	22	23	24	25	26	27	28	29	30	31

MAY
09
SAT

◑ ♒
Last Quarter 19º in Aquarius at 9:10pm (UTC)

Today is the Saturday to let go of a utopian ideal of community
life, drop an old habit or abandon your need to always have
the last word. Cutting yourself off from all this will help
you to connect on other levels in society, so enjoy!

MAY
10
SUN

☽ ♓
Moon in Pisces

F S S M T W T F S S M T W T F S S M T W T F S S M T W T F S S
1 2 3 4 5 6 7 8 9 10 11 12 13 14 15 16 17 18 19 20 21 22 23 24 25 26 27 28 29 30 31

MAY

11

MON

☉ ♉ ✳ ♃ ♋

Sun in Taurus sextile Jupiter in Cancer

The week begins softly – perhaps you are seeking to claim
your identity, even if you have to give up some things to
feel emotionally secure. Have a think about which emotion
brings you the greatest peace of mind and in which
relationships you feel most emotionally nourished.

☽ ♓

Moon in Pisces

MAY

12

TUE

☽ ♓

Moon in Pisces

MAY

13

WED

☿ ♉ ✳ ♃ ♋
Mercury in Taurus sextile Jupiter in Cancer

Now it's Mercury's turn to express his emotions more confidently. Discuss your plans with your family or support network. Talking about how you feel can encourage others to do the same. Take the first step.

☽ ♈
Moon in Aries

MAY

14

THU

☉ ☌ ☿ ♉
Sun meets Mercury in Taurus

This is a great Thursday to communicate your ideas to the world. Since the beginning of the year, your search for a more restful emotional place has led you to make solid plans for more peace and security. Today, you talk about your material goals and see the big picture. Congratulations on your latest achievements!

☽ ♈
Moon in Aries

F S S M T W T F S S M T W T F S S M T W T F S S M T W T F S S
1 2 3 4 5 6 7 8 9 10 11 12 13 14 15 16 17 18 19 20 21 22 23 24 25 26 27 28 29 30 31

MAY

15

FRI

☽ ♉
Moon in Taurus

MAY

16

SAT

 ♉
New Moon 25º in Taurus at 8:01pm (UTC)

It's New Moon Saturday, opening a new chapter in this area
of your birth chart. Reflect on your material life and evaluate
where you need more stability or resources. Do you need
more stability? Do you feel you have enough resources? Enjoy
good food and company that provides a sense of safety.

MAY
17
SUN

☿ ♊
Mercury enters Gemini until 1 June

After the Zodiac's most indulgent New Moon,
Mercury enters one of your houses and is ready
to make things happen with the right people.
It's time to reconnect with your best contacts,
catch up with friends and talk about your passions.
All intellectual endeavours gain momentum, so don't
let your focus and attention be wasted. Good luck!

☽ ♊
Moon in Gemini

MAY
18
MON

☿ ☌ ♅ ♊
Mercury meets Uranus in Gemini

Electric Monday looks pretty surprising. Your thoughts
may move quickly but not everyone can keep up
with your speed. Be careful not to stress yourself
out mentally or get carried away by anxiety.

♂ ♉
Mars enters Taurus until 28 June

Mars takes root in Taurus for the next 40 days. Your
mind is agitated, but your actions deserve a slow,
continuous effort to create more serenity. This is the
best time of the year to determine a consolidated
course for your resources, multiply your assets,
increase your income and cultivate your wealth.

☽ ♊
Moon in Gemini

רז

י·ה·ה·ה

Meditation for the month of Sivan
Scan with your eyes from right to left

T A U R U S

16 MAY – 8:01PM (UTC) – NEW MOON 25° TAURUS

Los Angeles (UTC –7) • New York (UTC –4) • London (UTC +1)
Paris (UTC +2) • Sydney (UTC +10)

IN THE NEXT SIX MONTHS I WILL MANIFEST ...

_____

_____

_____

_____

_____

_____

_____

_____

_____

Safety	Stability	Sensuality
Productivity	Financial resources	Self-esteem
Persistence	Intimacy	Body aesthetics
Values	Pleasure	Comfort

☿ Ⅱ ✳ Ψ ♈
Mercury in Gemini sextile Neptune in Aries
A hectic day of dispersion and illusory dreams.
Let your imagination run wild.

♀ ♋
Venus enters Cancer until 13 June
Over the next 25 days, focus on your spirituality
and nourish yourself with self-love.

♀ ♋ ✳ ♂ ♉
Venus in Cancer sextile Mars in Taurus
Perhaps you feel more secure when you have a financial
plan in place. Try not to sacrifice your resources in favour of
achieving more emotional stability. Take care of yourself.

☿ Ⅱ △ ♇ ℞ ♒
Mercury in Gemini trine Pluto Retrograde in Aquarius
Despite today's anxious mind, think of who can best help with
your project and reach out to the key influencers in your life

☿ Ⅱ □ ☊ ♓
Mercury in Gemini squares North Node in Pisces
Meditate on your contacts to find the proper person to connect with.

☽ ♋
Moon in Cancer

MAY
19
TUE

MAY
20
WED

☽ ♋
Moon in Cancer

MAY
21
THU

☉ ♊
Sun enters Gemini at 12:37am (UTC)

The most agitated week of the year so far had to end with the
Sun in Gemini. This is the best time for all exchanges, interactions,
communications, learning and meetings. The Sun in Gemini reports
to Mercury that it's time to activate your network of friends and
introduce the right people to each other. The party is about to start!

☽ ♌
Moon in Leo

MAY
22
FRI

♀ ♋ □ ♆ ♈
Venus in Cancer squares Neptune in Aries

Venus' desire for spiritual connections are challenged by Neptune's illusions,
leading to possible disappointments. You need more genuine friendships.

☉ ♂ ♅ ♊
Sun meets Uranus in Gemini

It's the perfect day to connect with new, more interesting people. A party
or an online event could bring you the relationships you've been missing.

☿ ♊ ✳ ♄ ♈
Mercury in Gemini sextile Saturn in Aries

Mercury wants to introduce you to people who will prove important to you in the future.

♀ ♋ △ ☊ ♓
Venus in Cancer trine North Node in Pisces

Be open to receiving people into your life who are meant to come in and heal
relationships. Something or someone very beautiful could enter your life today!

☽ ♌
Moon in Leo

GEMINI

AIR

MERCURY

21 MAY
12:37AM (UTC)

GEMINI

MODE Mutable   **ELEMENT** Air   **RULING PLANET** Mercury

CRYSTAL Agate   **BACH FLOWER REMEDY** Cerato

PRINCIPLE Positive   **OPPOSITE SIGN** Sagittarius

GEMINI AND SIGNS IN LOVE

Aries	♥ ♥ ♥ ♥ ♡	Libra	♥ ♥ ♥ ♥ ♥
Taurus	♥ ♥ ♡ ♡ ♡	Scorpio	♥ ♡ ♡ ♡ ♡
Gemini	♥ ♥ ♥ ♥ ♥	Sagittarius	♥ ♥ ♥ ♥ ♥
Cancer	♥ ♡ ♡ ♡ ♡	Capricorn	♥ ♡ ♡ ♡ ♡
Leo	♥ ♥ ♥ ♡ ♡	Aquarius	♥ ♥ ♥ ♥ ♡
Virgo	♥ ♥ ♥ ♡ ♡	Pisces	♥ ♥ ♡ ♡ ♡

MANTRA I think   **POWER** Versatility

KEYWORD Communicate   **ANATOMY** Lungs, Arms, Shoulders, Nervous system

LIGHT

Social   Expressive
Curious   Inventive
Adaptable   Intelligent

SHADOW

Changeable   Restless
Ungrateful   Lacking
Stupid   concentration

MAY
23
SAT

◐ ♍
First Quarter 2º in Virgo at 11:11am (UTC)

After last night's party, it's time to cleanse your
life of relationships that are out of balance.
Don't blame yourself for not wanting to have
your energy drained. Detoxify yourself!

MAY
24
SUN

♂ ♉ ✳ ☊ ♓
Mars in Taurus sextile North Node in Pisces

This is a Sunday to welcome all that the
Universe has in store for you! Make an old
dream come true, enjoy moments of great
contentment and pleasure – you deserve
to live the life you asked the cosmos for!

☽ ♍
Moon in Virgo

MAY
25
MON

⊙ ♊ ✶ ♆ ♈︎
Sun in Gemini sextile Neptune in Aries

After a busy weekend, focus might be low. Today is not ideal for tasks needing full concentration, but your creativity and communication are strong. Make the most of it!

⊙ ♊ □ ☊ ♓
Sun in Gemini squares North Node in Pisces

Let your imagination flow in ways that are almost like meditation. Create a mind map of all the ideas that have inspired you recently and let yourself be guided.

☽ ♎
Moon in Libra

MAY
26
TUE

♂ ♉ □ ♇ ℞ ♒
Mars in Taurus squares Pluto Retrograde in Aquarius

Pay close attention to your financial plans so that you don't behave impulsively. Stick to your budget and don't get caught up in Uranian intemperance or you could end up losing everything on a bet with no guarantee of success.

⊙ ♊ △ ♇ ℞ ♒
Sun in Gemini trine Pluto Retrograde in Aquarius

Among the many new people you're meeting, there may be that special person who will give you the strength you need to reveal your best talents. Who will it be?

☽ ♎
Moon in Libra

MAY

27

WED

☽ ♎
Moon in Libra

MAY

28

THU

☽ ♏
Moon in Scorpio

MAY
29
FRI

♀ ♋ □ ♄ ♈
Venus in Cancer squares Saturn in Aries

Balance your independence with emotional needs. Avoid making commitments out of fear of being alone or isolating yourself to avoid vulnerability. Aim for a balanced approach.

☽ ♏
Moon in Scorpio

MAY
30
SAT

☽ ♐
Moon in Sagittarius

MAY

31

SUN

○ ♐
Full Moon 10º in Sagittarius at 8:45am (UTC)

We end this busy month with a Full Moon that celebrates
our adventures and our instinct to explore, learning
from situations that teach us about life. What's your
next big milestone? Celebrate all the risks you've
taken around a campfire in the middle of nature!

MON	TUE	WED
01	02	03
08 ◐ ♓	09	10
15	16	17
● ♊		
22	23	24
29	30	
○ ♑		

JU NE

The following are the planetary changes that will happen this month

MERCURY

MOVES TO ♋ 1 JUNE

VENUS

MOVES TO ♌ 13 JUNE

SUN

MOVES TO ♋ 21 JUNE

MARS

MOVES TO ♊ 28 JUNE

JUPITER

MOVES TO ♌ 30 JUNE

THU	FRI	SAT	SUN
04	05	06	07
11	12	13	14
18	19	20	21
			SOLSTICE
25	26	27	28

JUN
01
MON

☿ ♋
Mercury enters Cancer until 9 August (will retrograde)

The month begins on a Monday with Mercury diving into
Cancerian waters for a long transit, eager to understand
the emotional gears that work behind the scenes of your
life. It's an excellent time for internal investigation, to heal
emotional wounds from the past, research emotional
and physical histories and achieve spiritual upliftment.

☽ ♐
Moon in Sagittarius

JUN
02
TUE

☉ ♊ ⚹ ♄ ♈
Sun in Gemini sextile Saturn in Aries

It's time to take responsibility within a friendship group.
Perhaps your curiosity is leading you to take a more
independent position or your commitment to yourself
is stronger now than to others. Listen to others, but
channel your energy with discretion and discernment.

☽ ♑
Moon in Capricorn

JUN

03

WED

☿ ♋ △ ☊ ♓
Mercury in Cancer trine North Node in Pisces

Today, refine your internal analysis to uncover
the roots of your emotions or traumas that drive
your ambitions. Embrace all thoughts honestly
and confront your insecurities fearlessly.

☽ ♑
Moon in Capricorn

JUN

04

THU

☿ ♋ □ ♆ ♈
Mercury in Cancer squares Neptune in Aries

Face your illusions and acknowledge your weaknesses. This
is a crucial time for soul healing, so see the facts clearly
and avoid believing in the fantasies you have created to
protect yourself. Be careful and gentle with yourself.

☽ ♒
Moon in Aquarius

JUN

05

FRI

☽ ≈
Moon in Aquarius

JUN

06

SAT

☽ ≈
Moon in Aquarius

M T W T F S S M T W T F S S M T W T F S S M T W T F S S M T
1 2 3 4 5 6 7 8 9 10 11 12 13 14 15 16 17 18 19 20 21 22 23 24 25 26 27 28 29 30

JUN
07
SUN

☽ ♓
Moon in Pisces

JUN
08
MON

◑ ♓
Last Quarter 17º in Pisces at 10:00am (UTC)

After a week without many aspects but an emphasis
on internal work, this Monday is a chance for you
to put aside your wish for a different life and start
manifesting your dreams now. Stay in love with life
but try to make all your greatest aspirations a reality.

M T W T F S S M T W T F S S M T W T F S S M T W T F S S M T
1 2 3 4 5 **6 7** 8 9 10 11 12 **13 14** 15 16 17 18 19 **20 21** 22 23 24 25 26 **27 28** 29 30

JUN
09
TUE

♀ ☌ ♃ ♋
Venus meets Jupiter in Cancer

Today is one of the most auspicious days of the year when the great benefactor planets meet in the sky in the most nurturing sign of the Zodiac. Surround yourself with loved ones and with those who feed your soul. This is a day of great luck and protection for everyone!

☽ ♈
Moon in Aries

JUN
10
WED

☿ ♋ □ ♄ ♈
Mercury in Cancer squares Saturn in Aries

Maintain good communication in all your relationships. Set healthy boundaries with those you love the most and always protect your energy so that you never run out. By protecting your personal space, you will feel more and more emotionally secure.

☽ ♈
Moon in Aries

M	T	W	T	F	S	S	M	T	W	T	F	S	S	M	T	W	T	F	S	S	M	T	W	T	F	S	S	M	T
1	2	3	4	5	6	7	8	9	10	11	12	13	14	15	16	17	18	19	20	21	22	23	24	25	26	27	28	29	30

JUN
11
THU

☽ ♉
Moon in Taurus

JUN
12
FRI

☽ ♉
Moon in Taurus

M	T	W	T	F	S	S	M	T	W	T	F	S	S	M	T	W	T	F	S	S	M	T	W	T	F	S	S	M	T
1	2	3	4	5	6	7	8	9	10	11	12	13	14	15	16	17	18	19	20	21	22	23	24	25	26	27	28	29	30

JUN
13
SAT

♀ ♌
Venus enters Leo until 9 July

Venus enters Leo and she wants to look her best for a big party!
Nothing could be more deserved after all that gazing inward.
Now's the time to showcase your emotional growth, to believe in
yourself and be confident, and let your talents win over a crowd.

☽ ♊
Moon in Gemini

JUN
14
SUN

☽ ♊
Moon in Gemini

JUN
15
MON

♀ ♌ ✳ ♅ ♊
Venus in Leo sextile Uranus in Gemini

Confidence is growing and now Venus is tackling
the digital realm. It's a great time for creating
a study group, pooling talents and talking
about art and creativity. Find your gang!

● ♊
New Moon 24º in Gemini at 2:54am (UTC)

The New Moon in Gemini is a sign of a fresh
stage in friendships. Joining a class, a course or
a workshop would be an ideal way to direct this
energy of new beginnings into communication.
It's time to learn a novel skill or practise an
old one with the people of your choice.

☽ ♋
Moon in Cancer

JUN
16
TUE

☽ ♋
Moon in Cancer

JUN
17
WED

♀ ♌ △ ♆ ♈
Venus in Leo trine Neptune in Aries

This aspect calls for you to be cautious about putting yourself in the spotlight for the sake of drama, rather than for your own creativity and achievements. Shine like a diamond but with your feet firmly on the ground.

♀ ♌ ☌ ♇ ℞ ♒
Venus in Leo opposite Pluto Retrograde in Aquarius

Once again, reveal your treasures in a controlled, restricted way and to a select few. All it takes is for one big figure to notice you and you'll be at the top of your game once again. Don't make a fuss – when Pluto faces Venus, he wants the stage all to himself!

☽ ♌
Moon in Leo

JUN
18
THU

☽ ♌
Moon in Leo

זהת

ה‧ו‧ה‧י

Meditation for the month of Tammuz
Scan with your eyes from right to left

GEMINI

15 JUNE – 2:54AM (UTC) – NEW MOON 24° GEMINI

Los Angeles (UTC –7) • New York (UTC –4) • London (UTC +1)

Paris (UTC +2) • Sydney (UTC +10)

IN THE NEXT SIX MONTHS I WILL MANIFEST ...

_____

_____

_____

_____

_____

_____

_____

_____

Flexibility	Social work	Connecting people
Adaptability	Curiosity	Learning
Cunning	Communication	Self-expression
Persuasion	Quickness	Youth

JUN
19
FRI

☽ ♍
Moon in Virgo

JUN
20
SAT

♅ ♊ □ ☊ ♓
Uranus in Gemini squares North Node in Pisces

Predestined news! You find the missing piece of a puzzle
when destiny comes to you in the form of a message or
a website. Whenever the planets aspect the North Node,
we get a brief glimpse into the inherent truth of our
reality here on Earth. Be aware of destiny's surprises.

☽ ♍
Moon in Virgo

JUN
21
SUN

☉ ♋
Sun enters Cancer at 8:24am (UTC)

This is a wonderful Sunday to celebrate a new season,
especially of the heart. When the Sun enters Cancer,
we want to be surrounded by care and affection.
Love and friendships are blooming and knocking
on your door to give you a fresh start. Welcome to
the most heart-warming season of the year!

Solstices
Summer Solstice – Northern Hemisphere
Winter Solstice – Southern Hemisphere
Litha – Celebrate life, light the fire in your heart!

◑ ♎
First Quarter 0º in Libra at 9:55pm (UTC)

The Universe urges you to reset your relationships.
Reassess what you're holding on to out of
need or convenience and make space for new
connections and a rebalanced heart.

JUN
22
MON

☽ ♎
Moon in Libra

M T W T F S S M T W T F S S M T W T F S S M T W T F S S M T
1 2 3 4 5 6 7 8 9 10 11 12 13 14 15 16 17 18 19 20 21 22 23 24 25 26 27 28 29 30

CANCER

WATER

MOON

21 JUNE
8:24AM (UTC)

CANCER

MODE Cardinal   **ELEMENT** Water   **RULING PLANET** Moon

CRYSTAL Moonstone   **BACH FLOWER REMEDY** Clematis

PRINCIPLE Negative   **OPPOSITE SIGN** Capricorn

CANCER AND SIGNS IN LOVE

Aries	♥ ♡ ♡ ♡ ♡	Libra	♥ ♥ ♥ ♡ ♡
Taurus	♥ ♥ ♥ ♥ ♡	Scorpio	♥ ♥ ♥ ♥ ♥
Gemini	♥ ♡ ♡ ♡ ♡	Sagittarius	♥ ♡ ♡ ♡ ♡
Cancer	♥ ♥ ♥ ♥ ♡	Capricorn	♥ ♥ ♥ ♥ ♡
Leo	♥ ♥ ♥ ♡ ♡	Aquarius	♥ ♥ ♡ ♡ ♡
Virgo	♥ ♥ ♥ ♥ ♡	Pisces	♥ ♥ ♥ ♥ ♥

MANTRA I feel   **POWER** Devotion

KEYWORD Feeling   **ANATOMY** Stomach, Pancreas, Chest

LIGHT

Tenacious	Friendly
Maternal	Emotional
Sensitive	Patriotic
Retentive	Traditional
Helpful to others	Good memory

SHADOW

Touchy	Lazy
Hurts easily	Selfish
Negative	Self-pitying
Manipulative	Insecure
Too cautious	Passive

JUN
23
TUE

☽ ♎︎
Moon in Libra

JUN
24
WED

☉ ♋︎ △ ☊ ♓︎
Sun in Cancer trine North Node in Pisces

This is a Wednesday that will be written in the stars. Follow your heart and be attentive to your emotions because today something subtle but also predestined to appear in your life may come to your attention.

☽ ♏︎
Moon in Scorpio

M T W T F S S M T W T F S S M T W T F S S M T W T F S S M T
1 2 3 4 5 **6 7** 8 9 10 11 12 **13 14** 15 16 17 18 19 **20 21** 22 23 24 25 26 **27 28** 29 30

JUN
25
THU

♀ ♌ △ ♄ ♈
Venus in Leo trine Saturn in Aries

As a gift from heaven, Venus has the chance to
restructure her future today with a more individualistic
vision, so she can shine even brighter. Think
about your true desires and you may receive a
divine sign today that triumph is within reach.

☉ ♋ □ ♆ ♈
Sun in Cancer squares Neptune in Aries

A stroke of luck can easily sweep you off your feet and
make your imagination and heart soar. It's a good time
to take off your rose-tinted glasses and understand
that without a plan, any dream is merely a fantasy.

☽ ♏
Moon in Scorpio

JUN
26
FRI

☽ ♐
Moon in Sagittarius

JUN
27
SAT

☽ ♐
Moon in Sagittarius

JUN
28
SUN

♂ ♉ ✳ ♃ ♋
Mars in Taurus sextile Jupiter in Cancer

It's the last transit of Mars in Taurus and Mercury is about to go retrograde, so use the day to set realistic and meaningful goals for the next six months.

♂ ♊
Mars enters Gemini until 11 August

Mars enters a transit of more than 40 days in Gemini as it responds to a retrograde Mercury, which means that we will have 40 days of the dispersion of mental energy, loss of focus, lack of concentration and a lot of agitation. Try to focus on one thing at a time and finish everything you start.

☽ ♐
Moon in Sagittarius

M T W T F S S M T W T F S S M T W T F S S M T W T F S S M T
1 2 3 4 5 6 7 8 9 10 11 12 13 14 15 16 17 18 19 20 21 22 23 24 25 26 27 28 29 30

JUN
29
MON

☿ St ℞ ♋
Mercury Stations Retrograde in 26º Cancer

Get ready for the longest 23 days of the year.
This time, Mercury goes deep into analysing your
emotions. The sentimental wounds and insecurities
that were swept under the carpet resurface
for you to deal with them once and for all.

○ ♑
Full Moon 8º in Capricorn at 11:57pm (UTC)

The Full Moon helps you stamp your mark on everything
you've achieved this year. Celebrate your victories
with those who always support you. Accept the credit
and feel the satisfaction of a mission accomplished.
Your value comes from within and recognition
of your excellence happens at the best time.

JUN
30
TUE

♃ ♌
Jupiter enters Leo until 27 July 2027

Jupiter in Leo stirs up your love life and biggest projects,
encouraging you to pursue ambitious dreams and share
your talents. Enjoy this optimism and fulfilling experience
but avoid overindulgence and self-promotion. Let your
uniqueness shine while staying mindful of others.

☿ ℞ ♋
Mercury Retrograde in Cancer until 23 July

Being in charge of your own life makes you think about
everything you've had to face to get here. Take advantage
of today to heal everything that has caused you sorrow.
There is no success without trial and error. Every
step, happy or sad, has led you to this moment.

☽ ♑
Moon in Capricorn

MON	TUE	WED
		01
06	07 ◑ ♈	08
13	14 ● ♋	15
20	21 ◑ ♎	22 ☉ ♌
27	28	29 ○ ♒

JU LY

The following are the planetary changes that will happen this month

VENUS

MOVES TO ♍ 9 JULY

SUN

MOVES TO ♌ 22 JULY

THU	FRI	SAT	SUN
02	03	04	05
09	10	11	12
16	17	18	19
23	24	25	26
30	31		

JUL
01
WED

☽ ♒
Moon in Aquarius

JUL
02
THU

♂ ♊ □ ☊ ♓
Mars in Gemini squares North Node in Pisces

In the middle of so many events, Mars asks for divine help
to guide his steps so that he doesn't stumble on his journey.
A small shift in your attitude today can create something
great in the future – a bold move orchestrated in the stars
will bring you good results down the road. Believe it!

☽ ♒
Moon in Aquarius

JUL

03

FRI

☽ ♒
Moon in Aquarius

JUL

04

SAT

♂ ☌ ♅ ♊
Mars meets Uranus in Gemini

High spirits, attitude and electricity can be explosive
if combined in unequal proportions. Today marks
a big encounter in the house of Mercury, who is
grieving and healing emotional wounds. Be careful
not to pass on the past violence you've suffered. Don't
take your anger out on others – you're the source.

☽ ♓
Moon in Pisces

JUL
05
SUN

♂ ♊ ✳ ♆ ♈
Mars in Gemini sextile Neptune in Aries

After a tough week, Sunday offers calm. Try to meditate, reduce anxiety and engage in artistic activities. Music and social events are a good idea this afternoon.

♂ ♊ △ ♇ ℞ ♒
Mars in Gemini trine Pluto Retrograde in Aquarius

If you've asked nicely, it's possible that you'll meet a special someone with the power to transform your mood and raise your vibration today. If you are staying at home, try to think of someone important you'd like to exchange information with. Use telepathy to draw that connection into your reality.

☽ ♓
Moon in Pisces

JUL
06
MON

☉ ♋ □ ♄ ♈
Sun in Cancer squares Saturn in Aries

In a slightly needy start to the week, you crave real connections at work and in your private life, but your self-criticism tells you that this is just an excuse not to fulfil the task you're charged with. Believe that it is possible to receive the embrace from the Universe that your heart so desperately seeks. Say "I love you" to someone important in your life.

☽ ♈
Moon in Aries

W T F S S M T W T F S S M T W T F S S M T W T F S S M T W T F
1 2 3 **4** **5** 6 7 8 9 10 **11** **12** 13 14 15 16 17 **18** **19** 20 21 22 23 24 **25** **26** 27 28 29 30 31

JUL
07
TUE

Ψ St ℞ ♈
Neptune Stations Retrograde in 4º Aries

Neptune is preparing to get illusions out of the way and plant his feet on more spiritually connected ground. We'll have five months to strengthen our faith at this favourable time.

◐ ♈
Last Quarter 15º in Aries at 7:29pm (UTC)

This Waning Moon also helps us to abandon a more defensive posture in relationships. Let go ot your pent-up anger, drop your shield and give yourself the encouragement you need to be you again.

JUL
08
WED

Ψ ℞ ♈
Neptune Retrograde in Aries until 12 December

Neptune's retrograde brings a realistic perspective, making it the best time to reinforce spiritual practices. Use this period to dissolve illusions, re-evaluate goals and align with your true aspirations. Enjoy!

☽ ♉
Moon in Taurus

JUL
09
THU

♀ ♍
Venus enters Virgo until 6 August

Venus in Virgo is about cleaning out what you no longer want. It's an excellent time for a good relationship cleanse, as organizing your heart will give you more insight into who is really rooting for your success and who only wants you because of something you do for them. Say goodbye to toxic relationships. It's time to purify your emotions.

☽ ♉
Moon in Taurus

JUL
10
FRI

☽ ♊
Moon in Gemini

JUL

11

SAT

Venus in Virgo opposite North Node in Pisces

Venus wants an emotional detox – she would like to clean
up both your love life and your social life. Rid yourself
of abusive relationships once and for all, including
friendships. This is an excellent day for someone
important to introduce themselves to you. Be open.

☽ ♊
Moon in Gemini

JUL

12

SUN

☽ ♋
Moon in Cancer

JUL
13
MON

☉ ☌ ☿ ℞ ♋
Sun meets Mercury Retrograde in Cancer

This is the sign that you've already passed the halfway point, that you've understood what needs to be corrected, healed, welcomed and embraced. You've passed the recent relationship tests, so now it's time to put into practice what you've learned about communication and setting boundaries.

♀ ♍ □ ♅ ♊
Venus in Virgo squares Uranus in Gemini

This challenging aspect can appear as someone wanting to test the limits you've just set to see how much you've really detoxified your heart. Are you ready for your first reality check in your relationships?

☽ ♋
Moon in Cancer

JUL
14
TUE

● ♋
New Moon 21º in Cancer at 9:44am (UTC)

This New Moon invites you to embrace your emotions and be with those you love. Set intentions for how you want to feel and be treated and how to nurture key relationships. Establish boundaries, even with family.

☽ ♌
Moon in Leo

כט

ה·ו·י·ה

Meditation for the month of Av
Scan with your eyes from right to left

C A N C E R

14 JULY – 9:44AM (UTC) – NEW MOON 21° CANCER

Los Angeles (UTC –7) • New York (UTC –4) • London (UTC +1)

Paris (UTC +2) • Sydney (UTC +10)

IN THE NEXT SIX MONTHS I WILL MANIFEST ...

_____

_____

_____

_____

_____

_____

_____

_____

Nourish	Past memories	Cooking
Nutrition	Protection	Ancestral heritage
Sentimental	Self-preservation	Romance
Emotional patterns	Care for the home	Intuition

JUL
15
WED

♅ ♊ ✳ ♆ ℞ ♈
Uranus in Gemini sextile Neptune Retrograde in Aries

Be open to new ideas and unconventional approaches. Let your intellectual curiosity lead you to explore new media, communication methods and innovative solutions. It's the ideal time to plug into your inner vision of the future and express your spiritual ideas through creative means and technology. Present your faith on the web and connect with your soul family!

☽ ♌
Moon in Leo

JUL
16
THU

☽ ♌
Moon in Leo

JUL

17

FRI

☽ ♍
Moon in Virgo

JUL

18

SAT

♅ ♊ △ ♇ ℞ ♒
Uranus in Gemini trine Pluto Retrograde in Aquarius

This aspect brings an excellent period for introspection and personal transformation. Reflect on your deep-rooted beliefs and the power dynamics that need to be changed in your life and in the world. Advocate for and support social reforms that promote equality, intellectual freedom and humanitarian progress. It's a Saturday for those who dream big!

☽ ♍
Moon in Virgo

W T F S S M T W T F S S M T W T F S S M T W T F S S M T W T F
1 2 3 **4** **5** 6 7 8 9 10 **11** **12** 13 14 15 16 17 **18** **19** 20 21 22 23 24 **25** **26** 27 28 29 30 31

JUL

19

SUN

♂ ♊ ✳ ♄ ♈
Mars in Gemini sextile Saturn in Aries

Despite the diffuse energy, the week ahead deserves
your attention and some forward planning. Take
advantage of Sunday to set clear and achievable
goals. Divide larger projects into manageable tasks
in stages and tackle them in a systematic way.

☽ ♎
Moon in Libra

JUL

20

MON

♃ ♌ △ ♆ ℞ ♈
Jupiter in Leo trine Neptune Retrograde in Aries

A beautiful meeting of Jupiter with two of the greats
helping you to lead from the heart. Let your intuition and
inspiration guide your creative endeavours. Lead by example,
demonstrating how visionary thinking and compassionate
actions can generate positive change in the world.

♃ ♌ ☍ ♇ ℞ ♒
Jupiter in Leo opposite Pluto Retrograde in Aquarius

As you seek spiritual leadership, be mindful
of power struggles in relationships. Reflect on
power dynamics in your life and promote shared
leadership, valuing everyone's contributions.

☽ ♎
Moon in Libra

JUL
21
TUE

♃ ♌ ✳ ♅ ♊
Jupiter in Leo sextile Uranus in Gemini

Jupiter is the star of the week and you're so busy
that you may miss out on some good prospects for
improving your performance. Take advantage of
opportunities for learning and intellectual growth. Keep
an open mind so that you can meet new information
and experiences that challenge your thinking.

◐ ♎
First Quarter 28º in Libra at 11:06pm (UTC)

This Moon in Libra helps you seek out the best groups and
social activities to further expand Jupiter's energy. Today
is a good day to practise active listening and perceive
different points of view as you gather the information
you need to create your own unique world view.

JUL
22
WED

☉ ♌
Sun enters Leo at 7:13pm (UTC)

A big party in the sky like this is a good time to celebrate
your talents, play with your inner child and show
off your creativity to your new social circle. You can
already celebrate the new emotional bonds you've
formed after working so much at inner acceptance.
Plan a nice date this Saturday with someone special.

☽ ♏
Moon in Scorpio

♌

LEO

FIRE

SUN

22 JULY
— 7:13PM (UTC) —

LEO

MODE Fixed   **ELEMENT** Fire   **RULING PLANET** Sun

CRYSTAL Ruby   **BACH FLOWER REMEDY** Vervain

PRINCIPLE Positive   **OPPOSITE SIGN** Aquarius

LEO AND SIGNS IN LOVE

Aries	♥ ♥ ♥ ♥ ♡	Libra	♥ ♥ ♥ ♥ ♡
Taurus	♥ ♥ ♥ ♡ ♡	Scorpio	♥ ♡ ♡ ♡ ♡
Gemini	♥ ♥ ♥ ♥ ♡	Sagittarius	♥ ♥ ♥ ♥ ♥
Cancer	♥ ♥ ♡ ♡ ♡	Capricorn	♥ ♥ ♡ ♡ ♡
Leo	♥ ♥ ♥ ♡ ♡	Aquarius	♥ ♥ ♥ ♥ ♥
Virgo	♥ ♥ ♡ ♡ ♡	Pisces	♥ ♡ ♡ ♡ ♡

MANTRA I want   **POWER** Magnetism

KEYWORD Creation   **ANATOMY** Heart, Back, Spine

LIGHT
Vain
Idealistic
Ambitious
Creative
Generous
Romantic
Optimistic
Self-confident

SHADOW
Dramatic
Worried about status
Proud
Arrogant
Afraid of ridicule
Cruel
Pretentious
Centre of attention

☿ St D ♋
Mercury Stations Direct in 16º Cancer

Mercury's alarm clock is finally ringing and you want to
catch up with all your agreements, especially the emotional
ones. From tomorrow it will be easier to reconcile your
emotions and thoughts, to talk about what you are feeling
with the people involved and to let go of the past once again.

☽ ♏
Moon in Scorpio

☿ D ♋
Mercury Direct in Cancer

You learned a lot during this retrograde because it touched
strategic points in your heart. With all your emotional analyses
up to date, now is an excellent time to resume your research
and reach decisions on all the pending issues. With a calm mind
and a serene heart, there's no room for insecurity to slip in.

☿ ♋ ✳ ♀ ♍
Mercury in Cancer sextile Venus in Virgo

In your first conversation, Mercury catches up with Venus
to confirm your desire to stay out of trouble in relationships.
It's another day to check your internal commitment to not
allowing abusive emotions and situations into your life.

☽ ♐
Moon in Sagittarius

JUL
25
SAT

Ψ ℞ ♈ ✶ ♇ ℞ ♒

Neptune Retrograde in Aries sextile
Pluto Retrograde in Aquarius

It's a magical Saturday for spiritual retreats.
Use Neptune and Pluto retrograde to gain deep
psychological insights. Engage in therapy, shadow
work or novel spiritual practices to uncover and
heal subconscious issues. Embrace self-discovery
and explore new forms of spiritual expressions.

☽ ♐

Moon in Sagittarius

JUL
26
SUN

♄ St ℞ ♈

Saturn Stations Retrograde in 15º Aries

Saturn is preparing to review your commitments, update
your responsibilities and re-evaluate all the agreements you
have made so far. We will have just over four months for this
meticulous work, which must be done with excellence and
as perfectly as possible. Get ready to fulfil this obligation.

☽ ♑

Moon in Capricorn

♌ ♒ ♌ ♌
The Node Axis changes to Aquarius/Leo
The South Node in Leo encourages you to let go of pride
and embrace authenticity. The North Node in Aquarius
promotes humanitarian efforts and social justice.

JUL
27
MON

♄ ℞ ♈
Saturn Retrograde in Aries until 10 December
Complete existing agreements before taking on new responsibilities.

☉ ♌ ☍ ♇ ♒
Sun in Leo opposite Pluto in Aquarius
Beware of power struggles, especially in leadership roles or group dynamics.

☉ ♌ △ ♆ ♈
Sun in Leo trine Neptune in Aries
It's a good day for intuitive leadership.

☉ ♌ ✳ ♅ ♊
Sun in Leo sextile Uranus in Gemini
It's time to trust your intuition, embrace new ideas and
transform personal and collective realities.

☽ ♑
Moon in Capricorn

JUL
28
TUE

☽ ♑
Moon in Capricorn

JUL
29
WED

♀ ♍ □ ♂ ♊
Venus in Virgo squares Mars in Gemini

The cosmic couple are in a challenging conversation as Venus wants to work on the relationship while Mars wants to socialize. Explore deeper aspects of your relationship and find ways to support each other's needs.

☉ ♂ ♃ ♌
Sun meets Jupiter in Leo

Today is excellent for setting ambitious, long-term goals. Focus on growth and development in your career, education or personal life. Stay positive and hopeful, even when facing challenges.

○ ♒
Full Moon 6º in Aquarius at 2:36pm (UTC)

The Full Moon of Kabbalah. Today is the day to wear white and go dancing in the streets to meet the people destiny wants to bring into your life. Happy Tu B'Av!

JUL
30
THU

☽ ♒
Moon in Aquarius

JUL
31
FRI

☽ ♓
Moon in Pisces

MON	TUE	WED
31		
03	04	05
10	11	12 TOTAL ECLIPSE
		● ♌
17	18	19
24	25	26

AUGUST

The following
are the planetary
changes that will
happen this month

VENUS

MOVES TO ♎ 6 AUG

MERCURY

MOVES TO ♌ 9 AUG

MOVES TO ♍ 25 AUG

MARS

MOVES TO ♋ 11 AUG

SUN

MOVES TO ♍ 23 AUG

THU	FRI	SAT	SUN
		01	02
06 ◐ ♉	07	08	09
13	14	15	16
20 ◐ ♏	21	22	23 ☉ ♍
27	28 **PARTIAL ECLIPSE** ○ ♓	29	30

AUG
01
SAT

☽ ♓
Moon in Pisces

AUG
02
SUN

☽ ♈
Moon in Aries

S S M T W T F S S M T W T F S S M T W T F S S M T W T F S S M
1 2 3 4 5 6 7 8 9 10 11 12 13 14 15 16 17 18 19 20 21 22 23 24 25 26 27 28 29 30 31

AUG
03
MON

☽ ♈
Moon in Aries

AUG
04
TUE

☽ ♈
Moon in Aries

AUG
05
WED

☽ ♉
Moon in Taurus

AUG
06
THU

♀ ♎
Venus enters Libra until 10 September

After a few days of rest from the Universe, Venus enters one of her houses for a transit full of beauty, highlighting social events. Time to connect with people, attend art events, music concerts and birthday celebrations. Don't remain in the dark!

◑ ♉
Last Quarter 13º in Taurus at 2:21am (UTC)

On the same day, a Venus-ruled Moon tells you to let go of any belief, situation or person that prevents you from feeling safe to share your talents and your gifts. You deserve to have all the resources you need to shine in society.

S S M T W T F S S M T W T F S S M T W T F S S M T W T F S S M
1 2 3 4 5 6 7 8 9 10 11 12 13 14 15 16 17 18 19 20 21 22 23 24 25 26 27 28 29 30 31

AUG

07

FRI

☉ ♌ △ ♄ ℞ ♈
Sun in Leo trine Saturn Retrograde in Aries

As the eclipse approaches, use Saturn retrograde to reflect on your long-term plans and responsibilities. Align your goals with your values to let go of what no longer fits. Anything that isn't aligned will slip effortlessly out of your life.

☽ ♊
Moon in Gemini

AUG

08

SAT

☽ ♊
Moon in Gemini

AUG
09
SUN

☿ ♌
Mercury enters Leo until 25 August

Mercury now enters Leo for the big event of the week.
Consider what qualities are no longer serving you as an
individual or as part of the community. Think from a Leo
perspective – it could be excessive pride, a need for attention,
ego-driven behaviour or a focus on personal glory. Reduce
or even try to eliminate ego dominance this season.

☽ ♋
Moon in Cancer

AUG
10
MON

♀ ♎ △ ♇ ℞ ♒
Venus in Libra trine Pluto Retrograde in Aquarius

A few days until the eclipse, this big day is an invitation for
you to embrace a love that will change your life. Use this
moment to deepen your emotional connections and explore
the deeper layers of your relationships and personal values.

☽ ♋
Moon in Cancer

AUG

11

TUE

☌ ♊ △ ☊ ♒
Mars in Gemini trine North Node in Aquarius

Despite your lack of focus in recent days, you have a
growing desire to improve your knowledge. How about
looking for a study group with common interests or
organizations that align with your ideals and goals?

☌ ♋
Mars enters Cancer until 28 September

Mars in Cancer channels the energy of this transit through
your emotions and feelings. Be open to listening to your
inner voice and following your instincts, even if this means
taking a less direct route to achieving your goals.

☽ ♌
Moon in Leo

☿ ♌ ☍ ♇ ℞ ♒
Mercury in Leo opposite Pluto Retrograde in Aquarius
It's the most highly awaited day of the year and Mercury is
busy trying to avoid power dynamics in communications.

AUG

12

WED

☿ ♌ △ ♆ ℞ ♈
Mercury in Leo trine Neptune Retrograde in Aries
This is a great opportunity to embrace humility
and connect with the community.

♀ ♎ △ ♅ ♊
Venus in Libra trine Uranus in Gemini
Unexpected opportunities will attract new people and emotions
into your social life, enriching your experiences.

☿ ♌ ✳ ♅ ♊
Mercury in Leo sextile Uranus in Gemini
Trust in the synchronicity of events and allow
yourself to be guided by intuition.

● ♌
New Moon Total Eclipse 20º in Leo at 5:37pm (UTC)
Set intentions that align with your heart's desires and
focus on developing projects that bring you joy.

AUG
13
THU

☿ ♌ ✳ ♀ ♎
Mercury in Leo sextile Venus in Libra

Still under the effect of the eclipse, this is the best time to communicate your feelings and desires in romantic relationships. Plan meet-ups that incorporate both intellectual involvement and aesthetic pleasure, such as exploring art galleries, going to concerts or having deep and sincere conversations.

☽ ♍
Moon in Virgo

AUG
14
FRI

☽ ♍
Moon in Virgo

Meditation for the month of Elul
Scan with your eyes from right to left

LEO

12 AUGUST – 5:37PM (UTC) – NEW MOON 20° LEO

Los Angeles (UTC –7) • New York (UTC –4) • London (UTC +1)
Paris (UTC +2) • Sydney (UTC +10)

IN THE NEXT SIX MONTHS I WILL MANIFEST ...

_____

_____

_____

_____

_____

_____

_____

_____

Being Queen or King	Pride	Hair care
Shining with the heart	Generosity	Power
Talents	Self-confidence	Self-expression
Creative projects	Vanity	Individuality

AUG

15

SAT

☿ ♂ ♃ ♌
Mercury meets Jupiter in Leo

This is a Saturday to party and show off to the world.
Once again, watch out for relationships where there
are power plays or communication isn't clear and there
is constant drama. Focus on expressing your talents
and your feelings in the purest and most vulnerable
way possible. There is magick in tenderness.

☽ ♎
Moon in Libra

AUG

16

SUN

☽ ♎
Moon in Libra

AUG
17
MON

♂ ♋ □ Ψ ℞ ♈

Mars in Cancer squares Neptune Retrograde in Aries

On the positive side, this aspect can stimulate creative and spiritual exploration, leading to a deeper search of meaningful artistic or imaginative projects.

☿ ♌ △ ♄ ℞ ♈

Mercury in Leo trine Saturn Retrograde in Aries

Take the time to clarify your goals and intentions. Make sure your actions are aligned with clear and realistic objectives rather than illusory or idealistic dreams.

♀ ♎ ✳ ♃ ♌

Venus in Libra sextile Jupiter in Leo

Small acts of kindness and generosity can have a significant positive impact and create a ripple effect of goodwill. Share your time and talents with others and be open to receiving in return.

☽ ♏

Moon in Scorpio

AUG
18
TUE

☽ ♏

Moon in Scorpio

AUG
19
WED

☽ ♏
Moon in Scorpio

AUG
20
THU

◐ ♏
First Quarter 27º in Scorpio at 2:46am (UTC)

Face your fears as they may be holding back your potential. It's time to take decisive action and embrace transformation. Dive deep into research and investigation. Whether it's a personal project, a work-related task or an intimate matter, use this time to gather information and uncover hidden details.

☽ ♐
Moon in Sagittarius

S S M T W T F S S M T W T F S S M T W T F S S M T W T F S S M
1 2 3 4 5 6 7 8 9 10 11 12 13 14 15 16 17 18 19 20 21 22 23 24 25 26 27 28 29 30 31

AUG
21
FRI

♀ ♎ ☍ ♄ ℞ ♈

Venus in Libra opposite Saturn Retrograde in Aries

Dedicate yourself to finding a balance between your need for independence and your desire for harmonious relationships. Communicate openly and discuss your needs and expectations in relationships. Be willing to listen and compromise and recgonize that both give and take are important.

☽ ♐

Moon in Sagittarius

AUG
22
SAT

☉ ♌ ☍ ☊ ♒

Sun in Leo opposite North Node in Aquarius

This aspect challenges us to find a balance between fulfilling your personal desires and contributing to something greater. It's time to evaluate whether your actions are motivated by personal recognition or a genuine desire to make a significant difference in the world. The passage of the Nodes invites you to channel your creative talents and leadership skills into initiatives that benefit society or promote positive change.

☽ ♑

Moon in Capricorn

S S M T W T F S S M T W T F S S M T W T F S S M T W T F S S M
1 2 3 4 5 6 7 8 9 10 11 12 13 14 15 16 17 18 19 20 21 22 23 24 25 26 27 28 29 30 31

AUG
23
SUN

☉ ♍
Sun enters Virgo at 2:19am (UTC)

Now the Sun enters Virgo and there is another
pair of eclipses to close a great chapter in history.
This is a great time to cleanse and purify yourself,
spiritually, physically and mentally. Be prepared for a
significant and important makeover by the Universe.

☽ ♑
Moon in Capricorn

AUG
24
MON

☽ ♑
Moon in Capricorn

AUG
25
TUE

☿ ♌ ☊ ♒

Mercury in Leo opposite North Node in Aquarius

Mercury's latest conversation in Leo asks you to share ideas that promote inclusion, equality and diversity. Use your communication skills to advocate for social transformation and progress.

☿ ♍

Mercury enters Virgo until 10 September

Mercury in Virgo feels at home and ready to do all the necessary restructuring to create a more solid and detailed impact at this important moment of the eclipses. Focus on organizing your ideas and speaking only when necessary.

☽ ♒

Moon in Aquarius

AUG
26
WED

☽ ♒

Moon in Aquarius

♍

VIRGO

FIRE

SUN

23 AUGUST
2:19AM (UTC)

VIRGO

MODE Mutable   **ELEMENT** Earth   **RULING PLANET** Mercury

CRYSTAL Peridot   **BACH FLOWER REMEDY** Centaury

PRINCIPLE Negative   **OPPOSITE SIGN** Pisces

VIRGO AND SIGNS IN LOVE

Aries	♥ ♥ ♥ ♡ ♡	Libra	♥ ♥ ♥ ♡ ♡
Taurus	♥ ♥ ♥ ♥ ♥	Scorpio	♥ ♥ ♥ ♥ ♡
Gemini	♥ ♥ ♡ ♡ ♡	Sagittarius	♥ ♡ ♡ ♡ ♡
Cancer	♥ ♥ ♥ ♥ ♡	Capricorn	♥ ♥ ♥ ♥ ♡
Leo	♥ ♥ ♡ ♡ ♡	Aquarius	♥ ♡ ♡ ♡ ♡
Virgo	♥ ♥ ♥ ♡ ♡	Pisces	♥ ♥ ♥ ♥ ♥

MANTRA I analyse   **POWER** Practicality

KEYWORD Dedication   **ANATOMY** Intestines, Liver, Vesicle, Lower plexus

LIGHT
Diligent
Scientific
Methodical
Discerning

Demanding
Clean
Pursues
perfection

SHADOW
Critical
Stingy
Melancholic
Egocentric

Afraid of disease
and poverty
Difficult to please
Sceptical

AUG
27
THU

☉ ☌ ☿ ♍
Sun meets Mercury in Virgo

It's an excellent day for self-reflection. Use it
to assess situations objectively, identify areas
for improvement and make practical decisions.
Focus on self-evaluation, self-care, and lifestyle
adjustments for better wellbeing and efficiency.

☽ ♓
Moon in Pisces

AUG
28
FRI

☿ ♍ □ ♅ ♊
Mercury in Virgo squares Uranus in Gemini

This aspect brings sudden changes in perspective and
misunderstandings due to differences in communication styles.

☉ ♍ □ ♅ ♊
Sun in Virgo squares Uranus in Gemini

The Sun emphasizes stability and routine, but Uranus
seeks change and experimentation. There can be
a conflict between attachment to tradition and the
desire to adopt new methods and technologies.

○ ♓
Full Moon Partial Eclipse 4º in Pisces at 4:18am (UTC)

The last eclipse in Pisces closes a great chapter. Use this
time to release repressed emotions and past traumas
through journaling, therapy, meditation, silent reflection or
energy healing. This is a unique moment in your history.

AUG
29
SAT

☽ ♓
Moon in Pisces

AUG
30
SUN

☽ ♈
Moon in Aries

AUG
31
MON

♃ ♌ △ ♄ ℞ ♈
Jupiter in Leo trine Saturn Retrograde in Aries

We end the month with this great alignment: Jupiter and
Saturn coming together to guide you to express your
authentic self and pursue your ambitions with courage
and determination. While Jupiter encourages you to
explore new possibilities, Saturn provides a stabilizing
influence, ensuring that your growth is grounded in
reality and sustainable in the long term. This aspect helps
you build a solid foundation for your aspirations, ensuring
that you have the structure, discipline and perseverance
needed to withstand challenges and adversity.

☽ ♈
Moon in Aries

MON	TUE	WED
	01	02
07	08	09
14	15	16
21	22	23 EQUINOX ☉ ♎
28	29	30

SEP TEM BER

The following are the planetary changes that will happen this month

VENUS

MOVES TO ♏ 10 SEP

MERCURY

MOVES TO ♎ 10 SEP

MOVES TO ♏ 30 SEP

SUN

MOVES TO ♎ 23 SEP

MARS

MOVES TO ♌ 28 SEP

THU	FRI	SAT	SUN
03	04 ◑ ♊	05	06
10	11 ● ♍	12	13
17	18 ◐ ♐	19	20
24	25	26 ○ ♈	27

SEP
01
TUE

♂ ♋ □ ♄ ℞ ♈
Mars in Cancer squares Saturn Retrograde in Aries

You may feel a block when trying to achieve your goals. This is because Saturn retrograde asks you to review your responsibilities and adjust your actions so that they are achievable, realistic and in line with your soul mission. Seek support from friends and mentors, and be patient with the slower process.

☿ ♍ ✳ ♂ ♋
Mercury in Virgo sextile Mars in Cancer

Afterwards, Mercury talks to Mars to make planning upcoming actions even clearer and more objective. Even if things are unfolding slowly, use this time to organize your home and work life, creating systems that boost efficiency, harmony and productivity.

☽ ♉
Moon in Taurus

SEP
02
WED

☽ ♉
Moon in Taurus

T	W	T	F	S	S	M	T	W	T	F	S	S	M	T	W	T	F	S	S	M	T	W	T	F	S	S	M	T	W
1	2	3	4	5	6	7	8	9	10	11	12	13	14	15	16	17	18	19	20	21	22	23	24	25	26	27	28	29	30

SEP
03
THU

☽ ♊
Moon in Gemini

SEP
04
FRI

◑ ♊
Last Quarter 11º in Gemini at 7:51am (UTC)

This is a Friday to put all the hustle and bustle
aside and rest your mind and ideas. We have a
quieter week ahead and the energy is about to
change radically. Look at thoughts and practices,
habits and routines that no longer serve you
and say goodbye to them. Just breathe!

T	W	T	F	S	S	M	T	W	T	F	S	S	M	T	W	T	F	S	S	M	T	W	T	F	S	S	M	T	W
1	2	3	4	5	6	7	8	9	10	11	12	13	14	15	16	17	18	19	20	21	22	23	24	25	26	27	28	29	30

SEP
05
SAT

☽ ♋
Moon in Cancer

SEP
06
SUN

☽ ♋
Moon in Cancer

SEP
07
MON

☽ ♌
Moon in Leo

SEP
08
TUE

♀ ♎ △ ☊ ♒
Venus in Libra trine North Node in Aquarius

Venus invites you to cultivate balanced relationships
that align with your future goals. Collaborate with
like-minded people and share your unique vision.
Trust that the connections coming into your life
these days will guide you toward growth and
your great purpose for the next nine years.

☽ ♌
Moon in Leo

T W T F S S M T W T F S S M T W T F S S M T W T F S S M T W
1 2 3 4 **5 6** 7 8 9 10 11 **12 13** 14 15 16 17 18 **19 20** 21 22 23 24 25 **26 27** 28 29 30

SEP
09
WED

☽ ♍
Moon in Virgo

SEP
10
THU

☿ ♎
Mercury enters Libra until 30 September

Mercury emphasizes communication in relationships, making
you want to understand your other half just by looking at them.

♀ ♏
Venus enters Scorpio until 25 October (will retrograde)

Venus wants intensity and passion. With a focus on
emotional depth and sensitivity, you're learning to
understand your partner and those around you better.

♅ St ℞ ♊
Uranus Stations Retrograde in 5º Gemini

It's time to try to understand each other telepathically.

☽ ♍
Moon in Virgo

T W T F S S M T W T F S S M T W T F S S M T W T F S S M T W
1 2 3 4 **5 6** 7 8 9 10 11 **12 13** 14 15 16 17 18 **19 20** 21 22 23 24 25 **26 27** 28 29 30

SEP
11
FRI

♅ ℞ ♊
Uranus Retrograde in Gemini until 8 February 2027

We've had five months of stagnation in our technological progress. This movement happens every year and serves to improve our media and electronic devices. It's not a good time for digital launches or for buying new equipment.

● ♍
New Moon 18º in Virgo at 3:27am (UTC)

The New Moon in Virgo asks you to release past negativity, cleanse emotional and physical spaces, and prepare for new beginnings. Embrace the new year with a spirit of celebration and avoid judgement.

Rosh Hashanah

☽ ♎
Moon in Libra

SEP
12
SAT

☿ ♎ △ ♇ ℞ ♒
Mercury in Libra trine Pluto Retrograde in Aquarius

This is an excellent time for uncovering hidden truths and using your analytical skills to explore difficult issues. It's also the best time to practise your powers of persuasion. Use your skills to influence and inspire others.

☿ ♎ ☍ ♆ ℞ ♈
Mercury in Libra opposite Neptune Retrograde in Aries

Channel the imaginative and creative energy of this aspect into artistic or visionary projects. Allow yourself to dream but keep your feet on the ground.

☽ ♎
Moon in Libra

T	W	T	F	S	S	M	T	W	T	F	S	S	M	T	W	T	F	S	S	M	T	W	T	F	S	S	M	T	W
1	2	3	4	5	6	7	8	9	10	11	12	13	14	15	16	17	18	19	20	21	22	23	24	25	26	27	28	29	30

SEP
13
SUN

☽ ♎
Moon in Libra

SEP
14
MON

☿ ♎ △ ♅ ℞ ♊
Mercury in Libra trine Uranus Retrograde in Gemini

This aspect enhances creative thinking and effective
communication. Uranus brings surprising insights
and moments of clarity, leading to breakthroughs
and new approaches to old issues. Expect
unexpected but enlightening conversations.

☉ ♍ ✳ ♂ ♋
Sun in Virgo sextile Mars in Cancer

Today's energy facilitates activities that are constructive
and productive. It's an excellent time for projects
that require attention to detail and, at the same time,
emotional investment. You have more stamina and an
increased ability to work hard to achieve desired goals.

☽ ♏
Moon in Scorpio

Meditation for the month of Tishrei
Scan with your eyes from right to left

VIRGO

11 SEPTEMBER – 3:27AM (UTC) NEW MOON 18° VIRGO

Los Angeles (UTC –7) • New York (UTC –4) • London (UTC +1)

Paris (UTC +2) • Sydney (UTC +10)

IN THE NEXT SIX MONTHS I WILL MANIFEST ...

Detox	Self-improvement	Synthesis
Reliability	Purity	Retirement
Clear communication	Adaptability	Diligence
Alchemy	Mental agility	Skill

SEP

15

TUE

♀ ♏ □ ♇ ℞ ♒

Venus in Scorpio squares Pluto
Retrograde in Aquarius

Seek emotional healing by allowing yourself to
confront and release deeply rooted emotions.
This can be a period of significant emotional
recovery and growth if you are willing to face and
integrate your darker aspects. A conversation
today may also highlight conflicts between
innovation and tradition. Finding a balance
between these contrasting needs is crucial.

☽ ♏

Moon in Scorpio

SEP

16

WED

♆ ℞ ♈ ✷ ♇ ℞ ♒

Neptune Retrograde in Aries sextile
Pluto Retrograde in Aquarius

Since 25 July, these two greats have been trying
to understand each other to promote the release
of shadows and collective spiritual healing. Since
then, we've had many opportunities to access
our inner divinity to develop our faith. Reconnect
with your beliefs and consider how your spiritual
ideals can uplift both yourself and others. The
most powerful healing comes from within.

☽ ♐

Moon in Sagittarius

SEP
17
THU

☽ ♐
Moon in Sagittarius

SEP
18
FRI

☿ ♎ ☍ ♄ ℞ ♈
Mercury in Libra opposite Saturn Retrograde in Aries

It's no good when you can't speak your mind just because you're afraid of displeasing others. Find ways to voice your opinion and make yourself heard, even if your ideals go against what the majority think. Be yourself and defend your ideas with elegance.

◐ ♐
First Quarter 26º in Sagittarius at 8:44pm (UTC)

Take a risk and start planning a new journey of knowledge and culture. This is the time to look at the big picture before setting off. Where do you want to sail to in the coming months?

SEP
19
SAT

☽ ♑
Moon in Capricorn

SEP
20
SUN

Yom Kippur

☽ ♑
Moon in Capricorn

SEP
21
MON

☿ ♎ ✳ ♃ ♌
Mercury in Libra sextile Jupiter in Leo

This is a wonderful start to a week when you will be more optimistic and positive in all your communications. You can now see the whole picture and approach situations with a broader, more philosophical perspective. Great social opportunities arise as Jupiter's expansive energy increases the chances of successful interactions.

☽ ♒
Moon in Aquarius

SEP
22
TUE

☽ ♒
Moon in Aquarius

SEP
23
WED

⊙ ♎
Sun enters Libra at 12:05am (UTC)

As the Sun illuminates Libra, we say goodbye to another season. Today, light and shade – day and night – have equal weight, so it's the best time to identify which areas of our lives deserve more balance. The Libra season is excellent for strengthening relationships and developing a purer sense of the beautiful things in life.

Equinoxes
Autumn Equinox – Northern Hemisphere
Spring Equinox – Southern Hemisphere
Mabon Festival – Celebrate abundance
by baking a delicious cake

☽ ♒
Moon in Aquarius

SEP
24
THU

☽ ♓
Moon in Pisces

SEP

25
FRI

☽ ♓
Moon in Pisces

SEP

26
SAT

☉ ♎ ☌ ♆ ℞ ♈
Sun in Libra opposite Neptune Retrograde in Aries

A busy Saturday as you want to achieve perfection in all your relationships. But make an effort to distinguish between what is possible and what is only fantasy.

☉ ♎ △ ♇ ℞ ♒
Sun in Libra trine Pluto Retrograde in Aquarius

Pluto proposes a major transformation. Be open to change and free yourself from old habits that hinder your growth. Take back your power!

○ ♈
Full Moon 3º in Aries at 4:49pm (UTC)

A Full Moon like this is enough to get anyone out of the house! The energy is contagious and you may be acting on impulse, but a magnetic force wants to place you above your desires. It's great to look at your journey so far this year and see how you can express yourself more forcefully from now on.

♎

LIBRA

△
AIR

♀
VENUS

23 SEPTEMBER
12:05AM (UTC)

LIBRA

MODE Cardinal   **ELEMENT** Air   **RULING PLANET** Venus

CRYSTAL Sapphire   **BACH FLOWER REMEDY** Scleranthus

PRINCIPLE Positive   **OPPOSITE SIGN** Aries

LIBRA AND SIGNS IN LOVE

Sign	Hearts	Sign	Hearts
Aries	♥ ♥ ♥ ♥ ♡	Libra	♥ ♥ ♥ ♥ ♡
Taurus	♥ ♥ ♥ ♡ ♡	Scorpio	♥ ♡ ♡ ♡ ♡
Gemini	♥ ♥ ♥ ♥ ♥	Sagittarius	♥ ♥ ♡ ♡ ♡
Cancer	♥ ♥ ♥ ♡ ♡	Capricorn	♥ ♥ ♥ ♥ ♡
Leo	♥ ♥ ♥ ♥ ♡	Aquarius	♥ ♥ ♡ ♡ ♡
Virgo	♥ ♥ ♥ ♡ ♡	Pisces	♥ ♥ ♥ ♥ ♡

MANTRA I balance   **POWER** Harmony

KEYWORD Relation   **ANATOMY** Kidneys, Appendix, Lumbar, Adrenal glands

LIGHT

Cooperative   Artistic
Persuasive   Diplomatic
Refined   Sociable
Impartial   Elegant

SHADOW

Fickle   Undecided
Apathetic   Easily discouraged
Intriguing   Seeking peace
Grumpy   at any price

SEP

27

SUN

☽ ♈
Moon in Aries

SEP

28

MON

☉ ♎ △ ♅ ℞ ♊
Sun in Libra trine Uranus Retrograde in Gemini

This is a marvellous start to the week after a busy weekend. Reorganize your ideas and see how you can coordinate your projects without appearing indecisive. Be tactful and diplomatic.

♂ ♌
Mars enters Leo until 25 November

It's time to act with boldness and determination, to channel your actions toward higher ideas so you can achieve all the recognition you've been waiting for.

☿ ♎ △ ☊ ♒
Mercury in Libra trine North Node in Aquarius

This aspect offers an interesting way for the Universe to blow incredible and inspiring ideas into your ears. Open your senses to what the cosmos wants from you!

☽ ♉
Moon in Taurus

SEP
29
TUE

☽ ♉
Moon in Taurus

SEP
30
WED

☿ ♏
Mercury enters Scorpio until 6 December (will retrograde)

Mercury plunges into a transit of more than 60 days in
Scorpio and the emotional cleansing will be one of the
deepest yet. All work involving research and investigation
gains momentum. It's the best time of the year to take
off society's masks and gaze directly at your soul.

☽ ♊
Moon in Gemini

T	W	T	F	S	S	M	T	W	T	F	S	S	M	T	W	T	F	S	S	M	T	W	T	F	S	S	M	T	W
1	2	3	4	5	6	7	8	9	10	11	12	13	14	15	16	17	18	19	20	21	22	23	24	25	26	27	28	29	30

MON	TUE	WED
05	06	07
12	13	14
19	20	21
26	27	28

OC
TO
BER

The following
are the planetary
changes that will
happen this month

SUN

MOVES TO ♏ 23 OCT

○ ♉

THU	FRI	SAT	SUN
01	02	03 ◑ ♋	04
08	09	10 ● ♎	11
15	16	17	18 ◑ ♑
22	23 ☉ ♏	24	25
29	30	31	

OCT
01
THU

☽ ♊
Moon in Gemini

OCT
02
FRI

☿ ♏ □ ♂ ♌
Mercury in Scorpio squares Mars in Leo

Combine assertiveness and sensitivity to know
when to speak up and when to keep quiet.

☿ ♏ □ ♇ ℞ ♒
Mercury in Scorpio squares Pluto
Retrograde in Aquarius

Today, conversations may reveal hidden
motives and truths. Take advantage of
transformative conversations because
your perceptions will be deeper.

♂ ♌ △ ♆ ℞ ♈
Mars in Leo trine Neptune Retrograde in Aries

Despite the arguments, try to set goals that
align with your ideals and values. Use the
inspiration of the moment to pursue your
dreams with passion and determination.

☽ ♋
Moon in Cancer

♀ St ℞ ♏
Venus Stations Retrograde in 8º Scorpio

OCT

03

SAT

Venus is preparing for her plunge into the depths of Scorpio where she will search for her inner treasures and discover what lies behind her most hidden desires and values. Get ready to be reborn!

♂ ♌ ☍ ♇ ℞ ♒
Mars in Leo opposite Pluto Retrograde in Aquarius

This is an excellent aspect if the intensity is channelled constructively. You should be careful, as there is a risk of becoming obsessive or excessively fixated on certain goals or desires. It is important to maintain balance and avoid destructive behaviour.

☽ ♋
Last Quarter 10º in Cancer at 1:25pm (UTC)

Let go of sorrows and insecurities; it's time to access your inner power. Dry your tears and keep your best friends around you. Let go of your fear of getting fully involved in a relationship.

OCT

04

SUN

☉ ♎ ☍ ♄ ℞ ♈
Sun in Libra opposite Saturn Retrograde in Aries

Saturn retrograde brings a sense of limitation or blockage to personal initiatives and independence. This period can be challenging, as you are called to reflect on past responsibilities. This is the best time to analyse your commitments and ensure they are in line with your true values.

♀ ℞ ♏
Venus Retrograde in Scorpio until 13 November

We'll have 40 days to investigate what lies behind our wishes and desires. Venus prompts you to reassess your goals and feelings. Use therapy, meditation and introspection to delve into your subconscious. Have a good dive!

☽ ♌
Moon in Leo

T	F	S	S	M	T	W	T	F	S	S	M	T	W	T	F	S	S	M	T	W	T	F	S	S	M	T	W	T	F	S
1	2	3	4	5	6	7	8	9	10	11	12	13	14	15	16	17	18	19	20	21	22	23	24	25	26	27	28	29	30	31

OCT
05
MON

☽ ♌
Moon in Leo

OCT
06
TUE

☽ ♌
Moon in Leo

T F S S M T W T F S S M T W T F S S M T W T F S S M T W T F S
1 2 3 4 5 6 7 8 9 10 11 12 13 14 15 16 17 18 19 20 21 22 23 24 25 26 27 28 29 30 31

OCT
07
WED

☿ ☌ ♀ ℞ ♏
Mercury meets Venus Retrograde in Scorpio

This is the best day to evaluate your emotions.
Book a counselling session to better understanding
what's going on in your mind. Awareness of the
problem is the first step to finding a remedy.

♂ ♌ ⚹ ♅ ℞ ♊
Mars in Leo sextile Uranus Retrograde in Gemini

Sharing what's troubling you with a therapist will
help you see how simple it can be to solve an
emotional issue or get yourself the recognition
you deserve. Sometimes a professional ear can
offer the support you've been waiting for.

☽ ♍
Moon in Virgo

OCT
08
THU

☽ ♍
Moon in Virgo

OCT
09
FRI

☽ ♎

Moon in Libra

OCT
10
SAT

♀ ℞ ♏ □ ♂ ♌

Venus Retrograde in Scorpio squares Mars in Leo

This is a Saturday of emotional clashes. The aspect
puts you on the spot to find out if you really want to
commit to a situation or if you're just using this issue to
satisfy your ego. The same goes for people, projects and
relationships. Pay attention to what your intuition tells you.

● ♎

New Moon 17° in Libra at 3:50pm (UTC)

This New Moon is the breath of fresh air we need to start
a new phase in our relationships and social life. Anything
out of balance will surface to make way for something
new, aligned with your ideals. Use this time to reaffirm
your feelings with friends and close companions.

T	F	S	S	M	T	W	T	F	S	S	M	T	W	T	F	S	S	M	T	W	T	F	S	S	M	T	W	T	F	S
1	2	3	4	5	6	7	8	9	10	11	12	13	14	15	16	17	18	19	20	21	22	23	24	25	26	27	28	29	30	31

דלג

ו·ה·ה·י

Meditation for the month of Cheshvan
Scan with your eyes from right to left

L I B R A

10 OCTOBER – 3:50PM (UTC) – NEW MOON 17° LIBRA

Los Angeles (UTC –7) • New York (UTC –4) • London (UTC +1)
• Paris (UTC +2) • Sydney (UTC +11)

IN THE NEXT SIX MONTHS I WILL MANIFEST ...

_____

_____

_____

_____

_____

_____

_____

_____

Relationships	Harmony	My own opinions
Partnerships	Perfectionism	Justice and honesty
Commitment	Visual aesthetics	Elegance
Conciliation	My own voice	Charm

OCT

11
SUN

☽ ♏
Moon in Scorpio

OCT

12
MON

☽ ♏
Moon in Scorpio

OCT

13

TUE

☽ ♏
Moon in Scorpio

OCT

14

WED

☽ ♐
Moon in Sagittarius

T F **S S** M T W T F **S S** M T W T F **S S** M T W T F **S S** M T W T F **S**
1 2 **3 4** 5 6 7 8 9 **10 11** 12 13 14 15 16 **17 18** 19 20 21 22 23 **24 25** 26 27 28 29 30 **31**

OCT
15
THU

☉ ♎ ✳ ♃ ♌
Sun in Libra sextile Jupiter in Leo

An excellent aspect after a quiet week, which puts
you among people who will be important for your
growth. Join groups that can support your projects
and forge closer ties with people of your choosing.

☽ ♐
Moon in Sagittarius

OCT
16
FRI

♇ St D ♒
Pluto Stations Direct in 3º Aquarius

It's hard to believe that Pluto's plunge is about
to end. You're beginning to regain control and
confidence. Tomorrow you'll surface from the
depths with a new vision of the world.

♂ ♌ △ ♄ ℞ ♈
Mars in Leo trine Saturn Retrograde in Aries

Today offers an excellent way to regain ownership
of your business. Something that seemed out
of your control comes back more concretely,
and you can determine whether you want to
continue with the commitment or give up on it.

☽ ♑
Moon in Capricorn

OCT
17
SAT

♇ D ♒
Pluto Direct in Aquarius

It has been an intense few months working on
your inner power to contribute to a better world. Your
inner vision and confidence have been restored and
now it's easier to assume your role in the community
and strive for an even more inclusive planet.
Congratulations on surviving so much intensity!

☽ ♑
Moon in Capricorn

OCT
18
SUN

◐ ♑
First Quarter 25º in Capricorn at 4:13pm (UTC)

Your Sundays have been busy, but what better day than
this to calmly organize the next stages in building your
future? Plan strategically, see what steps you still need
to climb to achieve the recognition you dream of.

OCT

19

MON

☽ ♒
Moon in Aquarius

OCT

20

TUE

♀ ℞ ♏ □ ♇ ♒
Venus Retrograde in Scorpio squares Pluto in Aquarius

Pluto's first conversation after retrograding is with
Venus, who is in her house participating in an intense
therapeutic process. It is essential to access the different
aspects of the collective to create a new value base.
You need to acknowledge your worth and focus on
rebuilding your power so you can reach more people.

☉ ♎ △ ☊ ♒
Sun in Libra trine North Node in Aquarius

Your actions and motivations are being guided by a
higher consciousness. Today is the time to appreciate
the beauty in the world, to create scenarios where all
your senses are involved. It's a day to be inspired by art!

☽ ♒
Moon in Aquarius

T	F	S	S	M	T	W	T	F	S	S	M	T	W	T	F	S	S	M	T	W	T	F	S	S	M	T	W	T	F	S
1	2	3	4	5	6	7	8	9	10	11	12	13	14	15	16	17	18	19	20	21	22	23	24	25	26	27	28	29	30	31

OCT
21
WED

☽ ♓
Moon in Pisces

OCT
22
THU

☽ ♓
Moon in Pisces

OCT

23

FRI

⊙ ♏
Sun enters Scorpio at 9:38am (UTC)

Now the Sun enters the most magnetic sign of the
Zodiac for a great journey into your emotions. This is
already an intense season, but the presence of the Sun
can illuminate those hidden corners of your soul and
help you rekindle your inner light. Don't be afraid of your
shadows – everything beautiful is born through darkness.

☽ ♈
Moon in Aries

OCT

24

SAT

⊙ ☌ ♀ ℞ ♏
Sun meets Venus Retrograde in Scorpio

This is the Saturday to assess how much you've
been using your power in situations and with
people just to make yourself feel better. Be honest
about relationships where you feel superior or
inferior and observe any power dynamics at play.

☿ St ℞ ♏
Mercury Stations Retrograde in 21º Scorpio

Mercury's retrograde at this time is fundamental for
letting go of your more selfish motivations, your desire
to control others and your intrusion into other people's
emotions. Pay attention to how your words affect
others, especially those you view as less significant.

☽ ♈
Moon in Aries

OCT
25
SUN

☿ ℞ ♏
Mercury Retrograde in Scorpio until 13 November

Mercury has been in Scorpio's underworld for a while and it's time to go over the lessons of the last few days once again. Don't be afraid to look at your emotions and work on your insecurities. If you're finding it too hard, seek help.

♀ ℞ ♎
Venus Retrograde enters Libra until
4 December (first time 6 August)

To ease the intensity a little, Venus picks up on issues from the beginning of August, looking at your interactions and relationships to help you pinpoint any mistakes you've been making. It's an excellent day to review a conversation with someone where you felt you were not very well understood.

☽ ♉
Moon in Taurus

OCT
26
MON

○ ♉
Full Moon in 3° Taurus at 4:11pm (UTC)

This Moon in Taurus reminds you to look at everything you've achieved and to understand that your great value lies within – that if you take care of yourself there's no place where you feel unwanted. The greatest love is that which is born from within, however clichéd that phrase may be. Indulge your senses by going out for dinner, buying yourself flowers or taking a nice bath.

☉ ♏ □ ♇ ♒
Sun in Scorpio squares Pluto in Aquarius

It's not an easy Monday. With so many challenges facing you, the Sun wants you to focus on your selfish goals and not look at the impact you're having on your surroundings. Pluto once again draws your attention to the fact that we are sociable beings, and we need to work to ensure that personal interactions are beneficial to us and to the world. Come out of your shell!

T	F	S	S	M	T	W	T	F	S	S	M	T	W	T	F	S	S	M	T	W	T	F	S	S	M	T	W	T	F	S
1	2	3	4	5	6	7	8	9	10	11	12	13	14	15	16	17	18	19	20	21	22	23	24	25	26	27	28	29	30	31

SCORPIO

WATER

PLUTO

23 OCTOBER
9:38AM (UTC)

SCORPIO

MODE Fixed   **ELEMENT** Water   **RULING PLANET** Pluto

CRYSTAL Tourmaline   **BACH FLOWER REMEDY** Chicory

PRINCIPLE Negative   **OPPOSITE SIGN** Taurus

SCORPIO AND SIGNS IN LOVE

Aries	♥ ♥ ♥ ♥ ♡	Libra	♥ ♡ ♡ ♡ ♡
Taurus	♥ ♥ ♥ ♥ ♥	Scorpio	♥ ♥ ♥ ♡ ♡
Gemini	♥ ♡ ♡ ♡ ♡	Sagittarius	♥ ♥ ♡ ♡ ♡
Cancer	♥ ♥ ♥ ♥ ♡	Capricorn	♥ ♥ ♥ ♡ ♡
Leo	♥ ♡ ♡ ♡ ♡	Aquarius	♥ ♥ ♡ ♡ ♡
Virgo	♥ ♥ ♥ ♥ ♡	Pisces	♥ ♥ ♥ ♥ ♥

MANTRA I desire   **POWER** Intensity

ANATOMY Reproductive system, Sexual organs, Bladder

LIGHT
Motivated
Penetrating
Director
Determined
Scientific exploratory
Researcher
Passionate
Conscious

SHADOW
Vengeful
Temperamental
Reticent
Arrogant
Sarcastic
Suspicious
Jealous
Intolerant

OCT
27
TUE

☽ ♉
Moon in Taurus

OCT
28
WED

☽ ♊
Moon in Gemini

OCT
29
THU

☽ ♊
Moon in Gemini

OCT
30
FRI

☿ ℞ ♏ □ ♂ ♌
Mercury Retrograde in Scorpio squares Mars in Leo

It's another Friday when tempers fray. Avoid any
conversations that make you want to confront people.
The energy of the moment calls for more recollection and
introspection than argument and shouting. Every ounce of
your energy should be conserved and used to heal your
inner wounds and work on your insecurities. Don't waste
your time with those who bring out the worst in you.

☽ ♋
Moon in Cancer

OCT

31

SAT

☽ ♋
Moon in Cancer

T F S S M T W T F S S M T W T F S S M T W T F S S M T W T F S
1 2 3 4 5 6 7 8 9 10 11 12 13 14 15 16 17 18 19 20 21 22 23 24 25 26 27 28 29 30 31

MON	TUE	WED
30		
02	03	04
09 ● ♏	10	11
16	17 ◐ ♒	18
23	24 ○ ♊	25

NO VEM BER

The following are the planetary changes that will happen this month

SUN

MOVES TO ♐ 22 NOV

MARS

MOVES TO ♍ 25 NOV

THU	FRI	SAT	SUN
			01 ◐ ♌
05	06	07	08
12	13	14	15
19	20	21	22 ☉ ♐
26	27	28	29

NOV
01
SUN

♀ ℞ ♎ △ ☊ ♒
Venus Retrograde in Libra trine North Node in Aquarius

On this Sunday you'll have more clarity about
everything that's been happening. Today, you can
gain a great understanding of all the lessons you've
experienced. Surround yourself with inspiration
and be open to signs from the angels.

◑ ♌
Last Quarter 9º in Leo at 8:28pm (UTC)

The Moon helps you let go of all the drama you've
experienced, release a certain repressed pride and
encourages you to smile and play again. Your greatest
talent is your ability to laugh at life's challenges, to take
trials more lightly and not to take yourself so seriously.
Seize the moment and learn to be happy again!

NOV
02
MON

☽ ♌
Moon in Leo

S M T W T F S S M T W T F S S M T W T F S S M T W T F S S M
1 2 3 4 5 6 7 8 9 10 11 12 13 14 15 16 17 18 19 20 21 22 23 24 25 26 27 28 29 30

NOV

03

TUE

☽ ♍
Moon in Virgo

NOV

04

WED

♀ ℞ ♎ ✳ ♃ ♌
Venus Retrograde in Libra sextile Jupiter in Leo

Review the mistakes of the past and, with great
humility, admit when you weren't so nice to
others in your relationships. This exercise in
taking responsibility for your mistakes expands
your consciousness and boosts your light!

☉ ☌ ♀ ℞ ♏
Sun meets Mercury Retrograde in Scorpio

It may not feel like it, but we're in the middle
of a deep process that seems to be lasting an
eternity. It's easier now to correct what needs
to be revisited so we can move forward with
our transformation. Don't give up now!

☽ ♍
Moon in Virgo

NOV

05

THU

☽ ♎
Moon in Libra

NOV

06

FRI

☽ ♎
Moon in Libra

S	M	T	W	T	F	S	S	M	T	W	T	F	S	S	M	T	W	T	F	S	S	M	T	W	T	F	S	S	M
1	2	3	4	5	6	7	8	9	10	11	12	13	14	15	16	17	18	19	20	21	22	23	24	25	26	27	28	29	30

NOV
07
SAT

☽ ♏
Moon in Scorpio

NOV
08
SUN

☽ ♏
Moon in Scorpio

S M T W T F S S M T W T F S S M T W T F S S M T W T F S S M
1 2 3 4 5 6 **7 8** 9 10 11 12 13 **14 15** 16 17 18 19 20 **21 22** 23 24 25 26 27 **28 29** 30

NOV
09
MON

● ♏

New Moon 16º in Scorpio at 7:02am (UTC)

The New Moon brings a fresh start after all the traumas we have collectively felt. It's a time to end an emotional cycle, to close a painful door on our journey so that new characters and new attitudes can enter our narrative. Let go of past negative feelings and celebrate the resilience you've gained through recent challenges. Those who have treated their own shadows with care now find there are no more obstacles. Celebrate this new version of yourself!

NOV
10
TUE

♀ ℞ ♎ ✳ ♂ ♌

Venus Retrograde in Libra sextile Mars in Leo

After the storm comes the calm. It's already possible to glimpse a smoother path in relationships. It's a good day to get along with your loved ones, to talk to friends, to update your relationship status. Venus desires romance and Mars wants to be honoured for who he is. You both win!

☽ ♐

Moon in Sagittarius

Meditation for the month of Kislev
Scan with your eyes from right to left

SCORPIO

9 NOVEMBER – 7:02AM (UTC) – NEW MOON 16° SCORPIO

Los Angeles (UTC –8) • New York (UTC –5) • London (UTC +0) • Paris (UTC +1) • Sydney (UTC +11)

IN THE NEXT SIX MONTHS I WILL MANIFEST ...

Intensity	Empowerment	Surrender
Transformation	Hidden places	Deep unconscious
Magnetism	Sexuality	Transmutation
End of cycle	Ability to keep secrets	Rebirth

NOV
11
WED

♃ ♌ ☍ ☊ ♒
Jupiter in Leo opposite North Node in Aquarius

Blessings are coming your way, bringing a
chance for personal growth and recognition.
You deserve the chance to display your talent
to a wide audience. Take advantage of the good
fortune and vibrate with optimism again.

☽ ♐
Moon in Sagittarius

NOV
12
THU

☽ ♑
Moon in Capricorn

NOV
13
FRI

☿ St D ♏
Mercury Stations Direct in 5º Scorpio

This is a very lucky Friday the 13th, when the best of friends make up again after so much backbiting. There have been so many challenges that your confidence has been knocked, but today you can smile again at life. Perhaps you are still a little bit shy, but you are also sure that you've done your best.

♀ St D ♎
Venus Stations Direct in 23º Libra

It's been a challenging 40 days for your self-esteem and your emotional security, but this will certainly lead to healthier relationships in the future. Be prepared!

☽ ♑
Moon in Capricorn

NOV
14
SAT

☿ D ♏
Mercury Direct in Scorpio

It's time to make all the decisions that were waiting for your answer. Communication, negotiations and the truth are now clear. Say YES to your new life!

♀ D ♎
Venus Direct in Libra

Celebrate your renewed confidence by joining friends for a luxurious sensory experience. Enjoy music, the arts, fine food and culture – fill your senses with everything beautiful within your reach. Shine!

☽ ♑
Moon in Capricorn

S	M	T	W	T	F	S	S	M	T	W	T	F	S	S	M	T	W	T	F	S	S	M	T	W	T	F	S	S	M
1	2	3	4	5	6	7	8	9	10	11	12	13	14	15	16	17	18	19	20	21	22	23	24	25	26	27	28	29	30

NOV
15
SUN

♂ ♌ ☍ ☊ ♒
Mars in Leo opposite North Node in Aquarius

Some of your attitudes are not yet set, so maybe
by being contradicted today you'll better understand
what the Universe really wants you to do. Be aware
of any external demands that are made on you.

☽ ♒
Moon in Aquarius

NOV
16
MON

♂ ☌ ♃ ♌
Mars meets Jupiter in Leo

A powerful Monday, with Mars feeling the
most confident of all in this grand encounter.
Everything great you could ever dream
of could be within your grasp. Your great
attitude could be rewarded with luxurious
surprises. Just beware of being ostentatious
– the Universe likes humble people best.

☽ ♒
Moon in Aquarius

NOV
17
TUE

☉ ♏ □ ☊ ♒
Sun in Scorpio squares North Node in Aquarius

The Sun is busy in the last degrees of Scorpio and still attached with some conviction. But the divine gears have a way of showing you how to stay focused on your ambitions and shine for the whole galaxy to appreciate. Focus on being remarkable!

◑ ♒
First Quarter 25º in Aquarius at 11:48am (UTC)

Technological advances have connected us across the world. Today, we can join hands and do our bit to contribute to the future of the planet. Something very important is happening in society and you are part of it. Take the first big step in a global project.

☽ ♓
Moon in Pisces

NOV
18
WED

☉ ♏ □ ♃ ♌
Sun in Scorpio squares Jupiter in Leo

Jupiter wants you to expand your brightness, but this won't be possible if you're still introspective or focused on your own desires. Let go of old attachments or outdated ideas you have about yourself. We are constantly evolving and you can't be afraid to take risks now. Spread your wings and fly!

☽ ♓
Moon in Pisces

NOV
19
THU

☉ ♏ □ ♂ ♌
Sun in Scorpio squares Mars in Leo

Recent months have stirred up deep emotions and issues,
leaving you defensive and suspicious. Today, focus on your
goals and let go of lingering insecurities. Mars urges you to step
into the spotlight and embrace your true self with courage.

☽ ♓
Moon in Pisces

NOV
20
FRI

☽ ♈
Moon in Aries

NOV
21
SAT

☽ ♈
Moon in Aries

NOV
22
SUN

☉ ♐
Sun enters Sagittarius at 7:23am (UTC)

Today, we start the end-of-year race. Everything that was stagnant is now picking up speed and sometimes it's hard to keep pace with the stars. It's time to be optimistic, believe in life, share what you've learned, celebrate with friends and explore new paths. What's your final adventure of the year going to be?

☽ ♉
Moon in Taurus

S M T W T F S S M T W T F S S M T W T F S S M T W T F S S M
1 2 3 4 5 6 7 8 9 10 11 12 13 14 15 16 17 18 19 20 21 22 23 24 25 26 27 28 29 30

♐

SAGITTARIUS

△
FIRE

♃
JUPITER

22 NOVEMBER
7:23AM (UTC)

SAGITTARIUS

MODE Mutable   **ELEMENT** Fire   **RULING PLANET** Jupiter

CRYSTAL Citrine   **BACH FLOWER REMEDY** Agrimony

PRINCIPLE Positive   **OPPOSITE SIGN** Gemini

SAGITTARIUS AND SIGNS IN LOVE

Aries	♥ ♥ ♥ ♥ ♥	Libra	♥ ♥ ♡ ♡ ♡
Taurus	♥ ♥ ♡ ♡ ♡	Scorpio	♥ ♥ ♥ ♡ ♡
Gemini	♥ ♥ ♥ ♥ ♡	Sagittarius	♥ ♥ ♥ ♥ ♡
Cancer	♥ ♡ ♡ ♡ ♡	Capricorn	♥ ♥ ♡ ♡ ♡
Leo	♥ ♥ ♥ ♥ ♥	Aquarius	♥ ♥ ♥ ♥ ♡
Virgo	♥ ♡ ♡ ♡ ♡	Pisces	♥ ♥ ♥ ♡ ♡

MANTRA I understand   **POWER** Visualization

KEYWORD Explore   **ANATOMY** Hips, Thighs, Upper legs

LIGHT
Honest
Philosophical
Free lover
Athletic
Generous
Optimistic
Fair
Enthusiastic

SHADOW
Exaggerated
Chatty
Procrastinator
Self-indulgent
Brash
Impatient
Player
Recklessness

NOV

23
MON

☽ ♉
Moon in Taurus

NOV

24
TUE

☉ ♐ △ ♆ ℞ ♈
Sun in Sagittarius trine Neptune Retrograde in Aries

This is a wonderful aspect for re-establishing our
faith and broadening our imagination, so that we can
explore all the unfinished business before 2027.

♀ ♎ △ ☊ ♒
Venus in Libra trine North Node in Aquarius

The Universe may be putting you in touch with
situations and people that will be key to your
development next year. Be open to new friendships.

○ ♊
Full Moon 2º in Gemini at 2:53pm (UTC)

Celebrate this year's achievements with friends, share key
lessons learned, and meditate on your goals for the future.

S	M	T	W	T	F	S	S	M	T	W	T	F	S	S	M	T	W	T	F	S	S	M	T	W	T	F	S	S	M
1	2	3	4	5	6	7	8	9	10	11	12	13	14	15	16	17	18	19	20	21	22	23	24	25	26	27	28	29	30

NOV
25
WED

☉ ♐ ✶ ♇ ♒
Sun in Sagittarius sextile Pluto in Aquarius

Discover the missing force that can help you expand your ideas even further. Perhaps assistance from foreign lands will reach you, so open up and make it easier for others to get to know your intentions.

☉ ♐ ☍ ♅ ℞ ♊
Sun in Sagittarius opposite Uranus Retrograde in Gemini

Learn to translate your message and convey your ideas in other languages. Don't miss out on the opportunity to present your philosophy to other cultures and countries. Practise by learning!

♂ ♍
Mars enters Virgo until 22 February 2027 (will retrograde)

This will introduce a period of three months to catch all the little details that prevent you from performing your best in life. It's time to put each talent into place, organize your next moves and plan your next projects using the wealth of information you've gleaned. Then, in 2027, you'll be performing with excellence!

☽ ♊
Moon in Gemini

NOV
26
THU

☽ ♋
Moon in Cancer

NOV
27
FRI

☽ ♋
Moon in Cancer

NOV
28
SAT

♀ ♎ ✳ ♃ ♌
Venus in Libra sextile Jupiter in Leo

This is a Saturday to receive blessings from the cosmos
for your good inner work and renewed confidence.
It's possible that your new friendships will lead you
to meet someone exceptional who will make you feel
super special. Open yourself up to new emotions.

☽ ♌
Moon in Leo

NOV
29
SUN

♅ ℞ Ⅱ △ ♇ ♒
Uranus Retrograde in Gemini trine Pluto in Aquarius

On this Sunday, expect powerful technological advancements, especially in communication and social media. Uranus encourages innovative approaches, while the trine with Pluto favours transformative changes in how we connect and share information.

☽ ♌
Moon in Leo

NOV
30
MON

☉ ♐ △ ♄ ℞ ♈
Sun in Sagittarius trine Saturn Retrograde in Aries

The Sun wants to bring even more expansion of knowledge, but Saturn is looking for structure and internal discipline so that you can ground your identity no matter where you are. It's by working every day on your personal routine that you can achieve global recognition. Define your individual rules. Which practices increase your optimism and wisdom?

☽ ♍
Moon in Virgo

S	M	T	W	T	F	S	S	M	T	W	T	F	S	S	M	T	W	T	F	S	S	M	T	W	T	F	S	S	M
1	2	3	4	5	6	7	8	9	10	11	12	13	14	15	16	17	18	19	20	21	22	23	24	25	26	27	28	29	30

MON	TUE	WED
	01 ◑ ♍	02
07	08	09 ● ♐
14	15	16
21 SOLSTICE ☉ ♑	22	23
28	29	30 ◑ ♎

DE CEM BER

The following are the planetary changes that will happen this month

VENUS

MOVES TO ♏ 4 DEC

MERCURY

MOVES TO ♐ 6 DEC

MOVES TO ♑ 25 DEC

SUN

MOVES TO ♑ 21 DEC

THU	FRI	SAT	SUN
03	04	05	06
10	11	12	13
17 ◐ ♓	18	19	20
24 ○ ♋	25	26	27
31			

DEC
01
TUE

Last Quarter 9° in Virgo at 6:09am (UTC)

Let go of habits that no longer bring you results. From time to time you need to adjust your schedule so that your priorities increasingly strengthen your personality and not the other way around. Clean up your activities, look at those that no longer bring you satisfaction, organize your day-to-day life so that you can deliver everything you need to by the end of the year.

DEC
02
WED

☿ ♏ □ ☊ ♒
Mercury in Scorpio squares North Node in Aquarius

There is a thought, an attitude or a way of thinking that is still keeping you away from your divine purpose. Today helps you take a cold, hard look at your negative beliefs about yourself and your value, which are preventing you from contributing more to your own progress.

☽ ♎
Moon in Libra

DEC
03
THU

☽ ♎
Moon in Libra

☿ ♏ □ ♃ ♌
Mercury in Scorpio squares Jupiter in Leo

Don't be too pushy or attached to your resolutions.
The days ahead ask you to go with the flow and
not to take yourself so seriously.

DEC
04
FRI

♀ ♏
Venus enters Scorpio until 7 January 2027
(first time 10 September)

It's time to revisit the knowledge gained but this
time from a place of much greater confidence
and awareness of your own power.

♂ ♍ □ ♅ ℞ ♊
Mars in Virgo squares Uranus Retrograde in Gemini

Take the time to identify how you are too critical of yourself
and where your judgement has prevented you from learning
your lesson. Look at yourself through the eyes of a child.

Chanukah first candle

☽ ♎
Moon in Libra

DEC
05
SAT

Chanukah second candle

☽ ♏
Moon in Scorpio

DEC
06
SUN

☿ ♐
Mercury enters Sagittarius until 25 December

This is a Sunday of adventure, of exploring new
paths and meeting new people. How about escaping
to the mountains and enjoying landscapes that
show you how small and insignificant we are?
Contemplating divine creation brings us ancestral
wisdom and ignites the flame of faith in life and
the future. Light a candle for your guides.

Chanukah third candle

☽ ♏
Moon in Scorpio

DEC
07
MON

☿ ♐ △ Ψ ℞ ♈
Mercury in Sagittarius trine Neptune Retrograde in Aries

Your optimism helps you access new ideas, while your desire to broaden your horizons helps you reach places of great understanding and inner satisfaction. You may be planning an international trip or your curiosity about a new culture or language may open doors to an even greater expansion of consciousness. Release the arrow of wisdom and pursue the knowledge that fascinates you so much!

Chanukah fourth candle

☽ ♐
Moon in Sagittarius

☿ ♐ ☍ ♅ ℞ ♊
Mercury in Sagittarius opposite
Uranus Retrograde in Gemini

DEC
08
TUE

In times of so many transformations, be adaptable and open to change. The unexpected insights and disruptions brought about by Uranus can lead to positive restructuring processes if you remain flexible and willing to evolve.

☿ ♐ ✳ ♇ ♒
Mercury in Sagittarius sextile Pluto in Aquarius

Challenge existing beliefs and traditions. Use this period to question the status quo and explore new intellectual territory. Take advantage of the expansive energy to find new solutions to old problems. Become the master of your own narrative!

Chanukah fifth candle

☽ ♐
Moon in Sagittarius

DEC
09
WED

☿ ♐ □ ♂ ♍
Mercury in Sagittarius squares Mars in Virgo

Today, self-criticism may hinder your progress, so focus on clear, direct communication and avoid letting excessive judgement stifle your creativity.

♀ ♏ □ ♇ ♒
Venus in Scorpio squares Pluto in Aquarius

Today's situations will help you to stop falling into ego traps. You have the capacity to overcome challenges with confidence and high self-esteem. Talk like a boss!

● ♐
New Moon 16º in Sagittarius at 12:52am (UTC)

The New Moon was the missing ingredient we needed to access our inner faith. With the right mindset, you can create real miracles in your life. Even though you're involved in so many events, take time to discover what you wish to explore intellectually in 2027.

Chanukah sixth candle

DEC
10
THU

♄ St D ♈
Saturn Stations Direct in 8º Aries

Just before the year ends, Saturn wakes up from going retrograde to help you commit to the goals you want to set for the coming year. Take responsibility!

Chanukah seventh candle

☽ ♑
Moon in Capricorn

עב

ה · י · ה · ו

Meditation for the month of Tevet
Scan with your eyes from right to left

S A G I T T A R I U S

9 DECEMBER – 12:52AM (UTC) – NEW MOON 16° SAGITTARIUS

Los Angeles (UTC –8) • New York (UTC –5) • London (UTC +0)

Paris (UTC +1) • Sydney (UTC +11)

IN THE NEXT SIX MONTHS I WILL MANIFEST ...

_____

_____

_____

_____

_____

_____

_____

_____

_____

Global exploration	Spontaneity	Long studies
New directions	Search for truth	Investigation
Freedom	Physical exercises	Philosophy
Optimism	Overkill	Foreign cultures

ħ D ♈
Saturn Direct in Aries

DEC
11
FRI

Today, you get the green light for everything
you've yet to take on. Something – such as a
signature on an important document or anything
that requires long-term responsibility – presents
itself to you. There are no more excuses for not
stepping confidently onto the path that you have
built for your future. Decide with confidence!

☿ ♐ △ ħ ♈
Mercury in Sagittarius trine Saturn in Aries

Make a list of everything that warms your heart
and blows your mind. It's an excellent day to
create lists of new goals and achievements.

Chanukah eighth candle

☽ ♑
Moon in Capricorn

DEC
12
SAT

♀ ♏ ✳ ♂ ♍
Venus in Scorpio sextile Mars in Virgo

It's another favourable Saturday for relationships
because everyone involved knows exactly where
they stand. It's a good time to talk about future
plans. Describe in great detail what an ideal
relationship would be like for you and how you'd
like to conduct yourself and your interactions
romantically. Be honest with the one you love.

Ψ St D ♈
Neptune Stations Direct in 2º Aries

Neptune is about to wake up, which helps us dream
big. It's time to access new dimensions of reality.

☽ ♒
Moon in Aquarius

T	W	T	F	S	S	M	T	W	T	F	S	S	M	T	W	T	F	S	S	M	T	W	T	F	S	S	M	T	W	T
1	2	3	4	**5**	**6**	7	8	9	10	11	**12**	**13**	14	15	16	17	18	**19**	**20**	21	22	23	24	25	**26**	**27**	28	29	30	31

DEC
13
SUN

♃ St ℞ ♌
Jupiter Stations Retrograde in 27º Leo

It's time for some to wake up and others to go into hibernation. We have worked hard on advancing ourselves during this transit from July until now. Between now and April we will have time to digest everything we have achieved individually so we can share our wisdom with the world.

♆ D ♈
Neptune Direct in Aries

Neptune's inspiration is great for motivating you to be more spiritual than mundane. It's an excellent time to share your faith and optimism with those in need.

☽ ♒
Moon in Aquarius

DEC
14
MON

♃ ℞ ♌
Jupiter Retrograde in Leo until 12 April 2027

The expansion now turns inward. We have four months to achieve the magnitude and nobility that Jupiter wants from us. You are now reviewing lessons previously learned and gaining experience and confidence in shining your light and using your talents.

☽ ♒
Moon in Aquarius

DEC

15

TUE

☉ ♐ ✳ ☊ ♒
Sun in Sagittarius sextile North Node in Aquarius

The Sun is approaching the central point of the galaxy and this aspect helps you to bring even more divine wisdom to Earth. Meditate and ask your higher consciousness to guide you along the best paths.

☽ ♓
Moon in Pisces

DEC

16

WED

☽ ♓
Moon in Pisces

DEC
17
THU

◐ ♓
First Quarter 25º in Pisces at 5:43am (UTC)

On the eve of a blessed transit, this Moon brings
you compassion and a desire to help others.
With the holidays approaching, what activities
could you engage in to extend your sense of
community and philanthropy? Do a good deed
today, give your love to those who need it most.

☽ ♈
Moon in Aries

DEC
18
FRI

☉ ♐ △ ♃ ℞ ♌
Sun in Sagittarius trine Jupiter Retrograde in Leo

The Sun aligns with the centre of the galaxy and
Jupiter sends the consciousness to expand your
role here on Earth further. Your life mission, your
divine purpose, may be revealing itself to you at this
time. Meditate on your sacred contribution to life.

☽ ♈
Moon in Aries

DEC

19

SAT

☽ ♉
Moon in Taurus

DEC

20

SUN

☽ ♉
Moon in Taurus

DEC
21
MON

☿ ♐ ✳ ☊ ♒
Sun in Sagittarius sextile North Node in Aquarius

On another divinely inspired Monday, receive blessings
for all the efforts you've been making. Connect
your essence with the work still to be done.

☉ ♑
Sun enters Capricorn at 8:50pm (UTC)

And we usher in another season with the entry of
the Sun into Capricorn. It's time to focus on what we
need to build for our future, to commit to higher goals,
to work hard to achieve our dreams. What are your
aspirations for a dignified and secure future?

Solstices
Winter Solstice – Northern Hemisphere
Summer Solstice – Southern Hemisphere
Yule Festival – Celebrate by lighting candles
to bring back the bright days

☽ ♊
Moon in Gemini

DEC
22
TUE

☽ ♊
Moon in Gemini

CAPRICORN

EARTH

SATURN

21 DECEMBER
8:50PM (UTC)

CAPRICORN

MODE Cardinal   **ELEMENT** Earth   **RULING SIGN** Saturn

CRYSTAL Turquoise   **BACH FLOWER REMEDY** Mimulus

PRINCIPLE Negative   **OPPOSITE SIGN** Cancer

CAPRICORN AND SIGNS IN LOVE

Aries	♥ ♡ ♡ ♡ ♡	Libra	♥ ♥ ♥ ♡ ♡
Taurus	♥ ♥ ♥ ♥ ♥	Scorpio	♥ ♥ ♡ ♡ ♡
Gemini	♥ ♥ ♡ ♡ ♡	Sagittarius	♥ ♡ ♡ ♡ ♡
Cancer	♥ ♥ ♥ ♥ ♡	Capricorn	♥ ♥ ♥ ♡ ♡
Leo	♥ ♥ ♡ ♡ ♡	Aquarius	♥ ♥ ♡ ♡ ♡
Virgo	♥ ♥ ♥ ♥ ♥	Pisces	♥ ♥ ♥ ♡ ♡

MANTRA I know   **POWER** Vision

KEYWORD Imagination   **ANATOMY** Knees, Bones and Teeth

LIGHT

Cautious   Traditional
Responsible   Practical
Scrupulous   Economical
Professional   Serious worker

SHADOW

Selfish   Conventional
Dominating   Stubborn
Spiteful   Inhibited
Fatalistic   Searching for status

DEC

23

WED

⊙ ♐ □ Ψ ♈
Sun in Sagittarius squares Neptune in Aries

You may feel a little disconnected or only inspired to do what you like. Get involved in artistic projects or practise active meditation by decorating your home, beautifying your environment and maintaining an energy of optimism and faith in your life.

☿ ♐ △ ♃ ℞ ♌
Mercury in Sagittarius trine Jupiter Retrograde in Leo

Great ideas can emerge when you start practising your faith. Celebrate the end of the year with those you love the most, prepare a surprise for the people you live with or call friends together for a great ritual of renewal. Ask everyone to bring their candles to celebrate the last days of the year and the first of this new season together!

☽ ♋
Moon in Cancer

DEC

24

THU

○ ♋
Full Moon 2º in Cancer at 1:28am (UTC)

This is a Christmas Eve with an emotional and welcoming Full Moon. It's a time to snuggle up in the nest and be there for those who have been by your side and helped you overcome the challenges of the last few months. Prepare a beautiful feast – even if it's not your speciality, get in the kitchen and contribute to the nourishment for this special evening. Cheers to LOVE!

T	W	T	F	S	S	M	T	W	T	F	S	S	M	T	W	T	F	S	S	M	T	W	T	F	S	S	M	T	W	T
1	2	3	4	**5**	**6**	7	8	9	10	11	**12**	**13**	14	15	16	17	18	**19**	**20**	21	22	23	24	25	**26**	**27**	28	29	30	31

DEC
25
FRI

☿ ♑

Mercury enters Capricorn until 13 January 2027

Once the celebrations are over, Mercury is thinking ahead about how to achieve financial stability and have an even more bountiful harvest in 2027. Create lists of objectives – you need to start planning your goals for next year now!

☽ ♌
Moon in Leo

DEC
26
SAT

☿ ♑ □ Ψ ♈

Mercury in Capricorn squares Neptune in Aries

We're in the final stretch of a great chapter! Balance logic with imagination. Double-check details to avoid misunderstandings and ground your dreams in reality. Use creative means to channel inspiration and clarity.

☽ ♌
Moon in Leo

DEC
27
SUN

☽ ♍
Moon in Virgo

DEC
28
MON

☽ ♍
Moon in Virgo

DEC
29
TUE

Sun in Capricorn squares Saturn in Aries

The year isn't over yet and it seems that your
responsibilities don't want you to take a break.
Even if you're on vacation, take time to reflect
and plan what paths you should take to achieve
the recognition and security you dream of. Make
your list of New Year's resolutions now!

☽ ♍
Moon in Virgo

DEC
30
WED

Mercury in Capricorn squares Saturn in Aries

Saturn doesn't want you to go into next year unsure of
the path you wish to follow. This is another day when
your responsibilities can take you away from the peace
and quiet that the end-of-year break should bring. Better
finish your tasks before you go into airplane mode.

◑ ♎
Last Quarter 9º in Libra at 6:59pm (UTC)

The last Moon of the year helps you to let go of
people and social attitudes that no longer serve you.
This is an excellent time to overcome insecurity, trust
your intuition and move past indecision. Embrace
a new life where you control your future.

☉ ♑ △ ♂ ♍
Sun in Capricorn trine Mars in Virgo

DEC

31

THU

The last day of the busiest year of our lives! This is the best possible combination for you to reach a conclusion about everything you want and what you need to do to get there!

☿ ♑ △ ♂ ♍
Mercury in Capricorn trine Mars in Virgo

Create mind maps using recent insights, contact people who have been important to you and be present in the relationships that build your new personality.

♀ ♏ □ ☊ ♒
Venus in Scorpio squares North Node in Aquarius

Today you close another chapter of 365 days. Sometimes you may have thought you wouldn't make it, but all the lessons were important and have brought you this far. Welcome to the new you of 2027!

☽ ♎
Moon in Libra

DREAM LIST

IN 2027 I WILL ...

JANUARY

M	T	W	T	F	S	S
		1	2	3	4	5
6	7	8	9	10	11	12
13	14	15	16	17	18	19
20	21	22	23	24	25	26
27	28	29	30	31		

FEBRUARY

M	T	W	T	F	S	S
					1	2
3	4	5	6	7	8	9
10	11	12	13	14	15	16
17	18	19	20	21	22	23
24	25	26	27	28		

MARCH

M	T	W	T	F	S	S
					1	2
3	4	5	6	7	8	9
10	11	12	13	14	15	16
17	18	19	20	21	22	23
24	25	26	27	28	29	30
31						

APRIL

M	T	W	T	F	S	S
	1	2	3	4	5	6
7	8	9	10	11	12	13
14	15	16	17	18	19	20
21	22	23	24	25	26	27
28	29	30				

MAY

M	T	W	T	F	S	S
			1	2	3	4
5	6	7	8	9	10	11
12	13	14	15	16	17	18
19	20	21	22	23	24	25
26	27	28	29	30	31	

JUNE

M	T	W	T	F	S	S
						1
2	3	4	5	6	7	8
9	10	11	12	13	14	15
16	17	18	19	20	21	22
23	24	25	26	27	28	29
30						

JULY

M	T	W	T	F	S	S
	1	2	3	4	5	6
7	8	9	10	11	12	13
14	15	16	17	18	19	20
21	22	23	24	25	26	27
28	29	30	31			

AUGUST

M	T	W	T	F	S	S
				1	2	3
4	5	6	7	8	9	10
11	12	13	14	15	16	17
18	19	20	21	22	23	24
25	26	27	28	29	30	31

SEPTEMBER

M	T	W	T	F	S	S
1	2	3	4	5	6	7
8	9	10	11	12	13	14
15	16	17	18	19	20	21
22	23	24	25	26	27	28
29	30					

OCTOBER

M	T	W	T	F	S	S
		1	2	3	4	5
6	7	8	9	10	11	12
13	14	15	16	17	18	19
20	21	22	23	24	25	26
27	28	29	30	31		

NOVEMBER

M	T	W	T	F	S	S
					1	2
3	4	5	6	7	8	9
10	11	12	13	14	15	16
17	18	19	20	21	22	23
24	25	26	27	28	29	30

DECEMBER

M	T	W	T	F	S	S
1	2	3	4	5	6	7
8	9	10	11	12	13	14
15	16	17	18	19	20	21
22	23	24	25	26	27	28
29	30	31				

JANUARY

M	T	W	T	F	S	S
				1	2	3
4	5	6	7	8	9	10
11	12	13	14	15	16	17
18	19	20	21	22	23	24
25	26	27	28	29	30	31

FEBRUARY

M	T	W	T	F	S	S
1	2	3	4	5	6	7
8	9	10	11	12	13	14
15	16	17	18	19	20	21
22	23	24	25	26	27	28

MARCH

M	T	W	T	F	S	S
1	2	3	4	5	6	7
8	9	10	11	12	13	14
15	16	17	18	19	20	21
22	23	24	25	26	27	28
29	30	31				

APRIL

M	T	W	T	F	S	S
			1	2	3	4
5	6	7	8	9	10	11
12	13	14	15	16	17	18
19	20	21	22	23	24	25
26	27	28	29	30		

MAY

M	T	W	T	F	S	S
					1	2
3	4	5	6	7	8	9
10	11	12	13	14	15	16
17	18	19	20	21	22	23
24	25	26	27	28	29	30
31						

JUNE

M	T	W	T	F	S	S
	1	2	3	4	5	6
7	8	9	10	11	12	13
14	15	16	17	18	19	20
21	22	23	24	25	26	27
28	29	30				

JULY

M	T	W	T	F	S	S
			1	2	3	4
5	6	7	8	9	10	11
12	13	14	15	16	17	18
19	20	21	22	23	24	25
26	27	28	29	30	31	

AUGUST

M	T	W	T	F	S	S
						1
2	3	4	5	6	7	8
9	10	11	12	13	14	15
16	17	18	19	20	21	22
23	24	25	26	27	28	29
30	31					

SEPTEMBER

M	T	W	T	F	S	S
		1	2	3	4	5
6	7	8	9	10	11	12
13	14	15	16	17	18	19
20	21	22	23	24	25	26
27	28	29	30			

OCTOBER

M	T	W	T	F	S	S
				1	2	3
4	5	6	7	8	9	10
11	12	13	14	15	16	17
18	19	20	21	22	23	24
25	26	27	28	29	30	31

NOVEMBER

M	T	W	T	F	S	S
1	2	3	4	5	6	7
8	9	10	11	12	13	14
15	16	17	18	19	20	21
22	23	24	25	26	27	28
29	30					

DECEMBER

M	T	W	T	F	S	S
		1	2	3	4	5
6	7	8	9	10	11	12
13	14	15	16	17	18	19
20	21	22	23	24	25	26
27	28	29	30	31		

FORGET ME NOT

WWW / APP	LOGIN
PASSWORD	EMAIL

WWW / APP	LOGIN
PASSWORD	EMAIL

WWW / APP	LOGIN
PASSWORD	EMAIL

WWW / APP	LOGIN
PASSWORD	EMAIL

WWW / APP	LOGIN
PASSWORD	EMAIL

WWW / APP	LOGIN
PASSWORD	EMAIL

WWW / APP	LOGIN
PASSWORD	EMAIL

WWW / APP	LOGIN
PASSWORD	EMAIL

WWW / APP	LOGIN
PASSWORD	EMAIL

ANA · LEO

THE ASTROLOGY DIARY

2026

01 14

√

Dream, Plan and Manifest!

Every day, Ana Leo looks at the horizon in search of new directions, discoveries and answers. A yogini and student of Kabbalah, she is intuitive and curious about hermeticism and occult sciences; she sees in the art of astrology a powerful way to promote self-knowledge and human development.

With a degree in Design and a post-graduate degree in History, Ana studied Astrology at the Faculty of Astrological Studies in Oxford. She took classes with renowned teachers and was a disciple of the most important astrologer in Brazil: Mr Zeferino Costa.

In 2019, Ana launched her *Astrology Diary* for the first time, a true guide to manifest your dreams in real life. In the same year, she studied Astronomy at the Royal Observatory in Greenwich, London, and since then she has not stopped travelling the world.

Spending her time between Brazil, England, Portugal, Panama and Argentina, Ana seeks inspiration and information to add to her personalized services. With astral charts and tarot readings, she's always attentive to the planetary aspects of the moment, the qualities of each person and the characteristics of each group she serves.

Find out more: YouTube.com/analeo and Instagram @analeo

Don't miss out on next year's diary, available from all good retailers from 1 August!